Acknowledgment

To Barry Knight, without whom this project would have never come to fruition. Thanks for your guidance, inspiration, and encouragement throughout this entire process.

Dr. Kevin Elko

A Tribute...

A Tribute to the Victims and Survivors of September 11, 2001

There are a few days that are etched in our minds forever, for those who were living during each event, the day Pearl Harbor was bombed, the day President Kennedy was assassinated, and the day the Challenger Space Shuttle blew up. One of those days for me, and a good portion of the world, is September 11, 2001, the day of the terrorist bombings of The World Trade Center in New York City and The Pentagon in Washington, D.C.

Even as I witnessed the aftermath of the World Trade Center with my own eyes, my heart still froze in disbelief.

A few years earlier, I was relaxing at home in Pittsburgh on a Thursday evening when I was startled by someone frantically pounding on my door. I answered it and was alarmed by the screaming person on the other side of the doorway who alerted me that a US Air jetliner had just crashed a few miles from the Greater Pittsburgh International Airport. He told me to get up to the crash site as soon as possible.

I had trained in critical stress counseling but I honestly never thought I would have a need to use this training, until now. The training proved invaluable, as I spent that entire night in a US Air Club comforting people who waited in earnest for their family and loved ones to disembark from a plane that never landed at the airport.

I felt extremely proficient on the topic of critical stress counseling after that evening. I was subsequently called to Montoursville, Pennsylvania, where a group of high school French students and their sponsors from that area had taken off from New York on their way to France for a field trip. The trip only lasted a few minutes, however, as the jet failed somehow and crashed.

I have since diversified from critical stress counseling and have been working mainly in the performance enhancement area and have been addressing mostly professional sports figures and financial brokers. Due to the financial brokerage area of my practice, I have spent a great deal of time recently in New York City because of the abundance of financial brokers that work there.

As soon as I heard of the tragic incidents of September 11, I knew that I would be personally touched because I had frequently worked with Merrill Lynch, which was impacted due to the World Trade Center destruction. Merrill Lynch had lost a key broker who was meeting with some clients atop the Trade Center that day. They had a number of people who had lost family members and close, lifelong friends due to the tragedy.

Also, one of their buildings that sat across the street from the Trade Center was heavily damaged. Many Merrill Lynch personnel worked right across the river in New Jersey and personally witnessed the tragedy as it unfolded. I called Merrill Lynch and offered my services, to which they quickly accepted.

When I arrived in New York City, I was forever touched by something I experienced first-hand that I did not realize from watching the destruction on the television. I actually felt and sensed the spirit that existed as I visited over twenty different offices in Manhattan and New Jersey.

When I returned, many people said to me, "That must have been hard." The fact is I am extremely glad I made that trip because it healed me as much as it did the stricken people I spoke to that week. I cried when I was finished, but my tears felt good because they were tears from the kindness and resolve of the ordinary people who were put through extraordinary circumstances. Once again, I found that the human spirit is an incredible thing.

One woman I talked to lost her son. Her broker brought her to hear me speak. After my presentation, I approached the woman and asked her about her anger. She quoted Martin Luther King, "If you take an eye for an eye, you will all eventually become blind." I have heard that quote many times before, but never from someone who just needlessly lost her son.

I also spent some time with a woman whose boyfriend was unable to get out of the building on time. She was taking flowers to her friends in the Merrill Lynch offices who had also lost friends. I spoke to a young man whose best friend from childhood, and who was also his roommate, was an employee at Canter Fitzgerald, and he knew he would never see his roommate again.

I felt the pain and anguish, but I also felt healing. I knew that day that New York was already starting to heal because they had quickly figured out that they refused to be terrorized.

Some people were cooking and preparing food for the firemen and others were taking them water. Others were giving blood in record numbers. Wealthy brokers who are usually tightly scheduled every moment of their day were walking in the streets around "Ground Zero" washing faces of people who were covered with dust.

There was a gentleness people were showing toward each other, even by the supposedly roughest and toughest people in existence, who would have normally been misread, but turned out to be some of the most gentle and strong people imaginable. As President Bush stated, adversity introduced itself to New York and the town was of an uncommon spirit because they needed each other and they knew it.

It appeared to me there was something else the people knew that existed, freedom. The evil beings that committed this heinous act were not free. They were robots programmed to hate and to kill. We as Americans have taken a different look at what freedom really means. For some of us, it was our first real look at what freedom means and what being an American means, which is to be free to believe what we want to believe.

Even though the terrorists attempted to enslave the people of New York, people everywhere understood that they were the ones who were free and the terrorists are the prisoners of their own insanity, hate, and evil. As a result, New Yorkers decided that even in these awful circumstances, they were free to be broken if that is what they chose, but instead, they chose to rise up from the dust.

That evening, while I was counseling people in the US Air Club, there was a man sitting at the bar for hours wondering if his wife was still alive. Finally, at 3 a.m., an executive from US Air entered the room and announced that there were no survivors. When this man jumped up from his bar stool I realized how large he was. He proceeded to walk toward the executive with anger in his eyes. I thought about restraining him if he tried to physically attack the US Air employee.

As he continued toward the executive, he saw a woman out of the corner of his eye sitting in a chair off to his right, crying hysterically after hearing the news that her husband was gone. Immediately, this enraged man stopped in his tracks, changed direction, and suddenly turned toward the woman. He approached the grieving woman, dropped to his knees in front of her chair, and held her. Somehow, he knew what he needed at that moment.

It became clear to me at that moment that people in the city of New York had figured that out from the first moment the catastrophe took place.

Foreward &
Introduction

68

Foreward

Nerves of Steel is about freedom, freedom to choose how you are going to think and feel regardless of the circumstances. *Nerves of Steel* is a guide on how to be mentally tough when times call for it and how to stay focused on those things that are truly important.

Pearl Bailey said, "We see God all the time, we just don't recognize him."

This book is about helping you see the good in all you do and how to become what you were created to do and to be. Think of all those New York City firemen who ran into the burning buildings to try and save the lives of people they never met. When was the last time you even did something good for someone you know, let alone someone you never met?

Can you think of a better model to use as an example for the rest of your life? Let the good come out of your life and decide to serve. Life does not offer us any permanence. This fact became apparent upon hearing all the stories about victims in the World Trade Center and passengers on the hijacked planes who called their loved ones to say goodbye before the end came.

At the end of each day, you have one less day left in the rest of your life. Our bank account of life consists of steady withdrawals, no deposits. We can not earn any extra time. Therefore, the time is now for you to listen to what is inside of you and what really wants to be brought out by your creator. You may need strength and toughness to do just that, and there is no better way than developing nerves of steel.

AN INTRODUCTION TO DEVELOPING
NERVES OF STEEL

"Life is a card game in which everyone is dealt a hand they must accept. Their success will depend on their playing the hand as well as it can be played." - **Lord David Cecil**

How do you think? Are you discouraged, depressed, uninspired, undisciplined, or just plain living life from day-to-day without any guidance or direction? Do you feel inundated by stress? Do you feel there are not enough hours in a day? Do you feel your days are uneventful and without meaning? Do you sometimes feel you are in a funk and just do not care anymore? You are not alone. As a matter of fact, you would be the minority if you did **not** experience most of the emotions such as stress, anxiety, or discouragement at one time or another.

The elimination of stress has been the topic of discussion for a long period of time, yet the ability to eliminate, run from, or reduce stress has never been formally taught in schools. Think of all the time we spent learning about many subjects in school: algebra, history, social studies, geometry. These are great subjects, but how many times have you been able to use what you learned in history or algebra to help make your day-to-day life better?

While school taught us important things, school never really taught us how to think properly in order to make day-to-day life not just livable but exciting. We were never formerly taught how to develop real "nerve" either, nerve that would allow us to face each day with courage rather than with bewilderment. Through *Nerves of Steel*, you can focus on living your life instead of having your life live you.

You may be asking yourself how this will be done? You will be presented with life-improving technologies such as goal-setting techniques, motivation enhancements, and forgiveness strategies. *Nerves of Steel* addresses these and other life-changing concepts by explaining step-by-step processes necessary to guide you through the journey we sometimes refer to as life.

WHY DEVELOP *NERVES OF STEEL*?

Because after completing this life-management guide, you will realize how to:

- Corral the subject of stress and guide yourself through the step-by-step process of focusing on the task at hand similar to how successful athletes focus on the contest at hand.
- Focus during tense situations, whether raising children, playing the stock market, playing a pick-up basketball game, or just plain enjoying life.
- Develop mental skills to properly focus on goals in life.
- Motivate yourself to act on your goals.

Do you feel you are working a dead-end job? Is your relationship stagnant and uneventful? Do you ever tell yourself, "Why does this always happen to me?"

Instead of worrying about what could go wrong, by developing nerves of steel, you will possess enough character to focus on what could go right. By reading this book and taking action based on its advice, you will have the potential to develop such attributes as self-discipline, initiative, persistence, and the will to win beyond your wildest dreams.

You will also learn from *Nerves of Steel* the information and techniques needed to prevent you from cracking under pressure and guide you as you stay on course toward a purpose in life. If you have not found a purpose in life yet, this manual will also help you define one.

Nerves of Steel is more than a catchy book title. It is a system that teaches you how to stop wishing life was easy and instead, focus on how to grab life by the neck and pull it toward you. Nobody ever said life was easy, and life is too short to waste valuable time wishing it was. Instead, use the time developing your nerves of steel to focus on handling life's pressures with ease rather than running from life's pressures, which may cause stress, depression, or worse.

David McClelland, a researcher on performance and motivation at Harvard, wrote a paper in 1973 entitled "Testing For Competence Rather Than Intelligence." He believed that academic aptitude, grades in school, and advanced credentials do not predict how well people would perform on the job or whether they would succeed in life. Instead, he said a specific set of competencies, including self-discipline and initiative, distinguishes the most successful individuals from those who are merely "good enough." He believed that people who became over-achievers developed nerves of steel.

Thomas Alva Edison is said to have been the "Father of Inventors." Born on February 11, 1847, Edison received 1093 patents before he died at the age of 84 in 1931. He applied for 141 patents in one year (1882) and was granted 75 of them. Did you know that Edison only had three months of formal schooling, which he received at age seven? The instructors had such a terrible time with him because he was asking too many questions that they labeled him as "unteachable" and sent him home. Edison spent his life reading and teaching himself the sciences.

He routinely spent 18 or 19-hour days working on inventions in his labs, losing all track of time and not knowing whether it was night or day outside. He did not believe in having a clock in his laboratory and was hard of hearing due to a childhood accident, so his outside distractions were limited. Edison is quoted as having said that genius is one percent inspiration and ninety-nine percent perspiration.

When one of his labs burnt to the ground, instead of fretting over the loss of thousands of hours of work, he simply said that now he could forget about all his previous mistakes and start from scratch.

How did the "Father of Inventors" achieve such great success with only three months of formal schooling? How did he develop unwavering motivation? How did he focus his energy entirely on the task at hand? How did he recognize the internal voice of judgment and avoid self-pity? He knew how to think!

The qualities in which Edison injected into his life are examples of techniques taught in *Nerves of Steel*. You may not be the next inventor of a product as useful as the light bulb, but by developing nerves of steel, your life will take on new dimensions. By tackling stress and still living life to its fullest, you will improve yourself more and more each time in the process by strengthening your nerves of steel.

Everyone faces challenges in life, but some people run and hide from their challenges and others who embrace their challenges. If you know how to think about life in a way that energizes and empowers yourself, you can meet life head-on, instead of letting life run over you like a locomotive running over a penny left on the train tracks.

The basic foundation of the *Nerves of Steel* system is based on the same attributes Edison excelled in:

- Identify what **really** motivates you.
- Focus your energy exclusively on your motivating factors regardless of what happens during your day.
- Maintain the practices that keep you on the course of living life to its fullest, no matter how stressful you may think your life has become.
- Develop the *Nerves of Steel* way of thinking by recognizing your internal voice of judgment and avoiding self-pity.

Phase One of the manual will set a *Nerves of Steel* foundation and encompasses the first four chapters or "floors" of the book. The qualities of steel as a metal include unwavering, unbending, and unforgiving; an extremely powerful force is needed to bend or break steel, such as molten flame, intense explosions, or catastrophic weather conditions. Steel is also defined in the dictionary as a state of mind mirroring the qualities of steel.

Each chapter is referred to as a "floor" because you will be learning to design your life just as an architect designs a building. You can become that architect and build the life you have always wanted, but never thought you could, even if do not know how or where to start.

This book will teach you the qualities and techniques needed to develop the mind or nerves like steel, so you are not negatively affected by trivial, day-to-day nuisances. By exercising your nerves of steel, you are more likely to remain focused on what you consider important in life. You may not even realize at this time everything you consider important in life, but you will be shown the tools to do so in this manual.

Many anecdotes presented throughout the book will further

illustrate essential qualities needed for everyday life as well. Personal anecdotes will be noted throughout the book as well.

Research has shown that athletes who have excelled in their respective sport suffer the same amount of stress as those who have not excelled, but the achievers use stress as a motivating factor rather than a crippling emotion.

Michael Jordan, former star of the Chicago Bulls of the NBA, was usually depended upon to take the clutch shot. He admitted excelling when the stress of a desperate or critical situation was thrust upon his team. He once stated that he felt as if he slowed down time during those brief seconds of a game-deciding, last-second play, which seemed to move in slow motion for him while the opposing players, and sometimes even his own teammates were frantic. He was then able to focus clearly on making the buzzer-beating shot or the last-second steal.

In his final appearance as a Bull, Jordan calmly drained the last shot he ever took as a Chicago Bull to clinch another world championship for his team. Jordan used his nerves of steel to handle stress and achieve at one of the highest levels of any sports figure ever.

It is possible for you to develop the same zest for life as Jordan displayed for the game of basketball by developing nerves of steel.

Some people may think Jordan was born with his talent. What these people do not realize is the hours and hours of practice Jordan put in each day, or the time spent by Jordan as a teenager driving hours away from his home to play in basketball games against top competition.

Professional golfer Gary Player is another example of a person who excelled in a profession through thousands of hours of practice that took place behind the scenes from the galleries and the fans.

"I would do anything to hit a golf ball like you," someone once said to Player. He quickly answered, "Would you get up at 6 a.m. every morning and hit 1500 golf balls?"

Upon the man replying, "No," Player quipped, "Then you wouldn't do *anything* to hit a golf ball like me."

Eddie Chambers is a nineteen-year-old boxer from Pittsburgh, Pennsylvania. He is an up-and-coming professional heavyweight who has his sights set on one day being the heavyweight champion of the world. In order to support himself, he and his father, who is a former boxer, and also his trainer, get up at 3 a.m. every morning and deliver newspapers around Pittsburgh. By 9 a.m., "Fast Eddie" and his father are at the gym working out, but it is not a fancy Hollywood gym.

From the outside, the gym looks like an old abandoned school. There are no television reporters or multi-million dollar contracts swirling around yet, but that does not slow down Eddie. He is in the beginning stages of his climb to success, which are usually the hardest to climb, especially for Eddie, who has to literally train hard and then fight his way to the next floor. If he maintains his nerves of steel, he just might be the heavyweight champion of the world some day.

Personal anecdotes are scattered throughout the book that relate to the information presented in each chapter. Following each floor (chapter) in the book is a profile of someone who used his or her *Nerves of Steel* to improve or change their life around. These short stories are called "Profiles of Steel," which are followed by examples of self-defeating dialogue, called "Dialogues of Steel" accompanied by self-motivating dialogue to address each profile.

As you advance through *Nerves of Steel*, you may find yourself wanting to jot down ideas or concepts that come to mind, especially thoughts that seem to hit you like a flood light being turned on inside your mind. Never hesitate to record any thoughts you feel will help you advance in life. Recording your thoughts in a journal is the best way to keep a record of your revelations, thoughts, ideas, progress, and exercises you may find useful while developing nerves of steel.

About The Authors

About The Author

Dr. Kevin Elko, a noted performance consultant, has been contracted by the Pittsburgh Steelers, Miami Dolphins, New Orleans Saints, Philadelphia Eagles, and the Dallas Cowboys of the National Football League as well as the Pittsburgh Penguins of the National Hockey League. He has also consulted for the University of Pittsburgh and the University of Miami Athletic Departments and the Young Presidents Organization.

Dr. Elko was a lecturer to the Sports Medicine Fellows at the University of Pittsburgh and an adjunct professor at Marshall University. In addition to his sports-performance practice, Dr. Elko also serves as a consultant for corporate America, including companies such as Prudential Securities, American General Securities, Travelers' Insurance, Consolidated Rail Corporation, Merrill Lynch, Abbott Diagnostics, and Smith Kline Beecham.

About the Co-Writer

Stephen Flinn has earned bachelor's degrees in Sociology, Journalism, and Communications as well as certificates in English Writing, Professional Writing, and Web Authoring. He has also earned a Masters of Business (MBA) degree. He has been a freelance writer since 1990, a staff writer for various magazines and newspapers, and has published several hundred pieces to date nationwide.

Nerves of Steel is their first joint project.

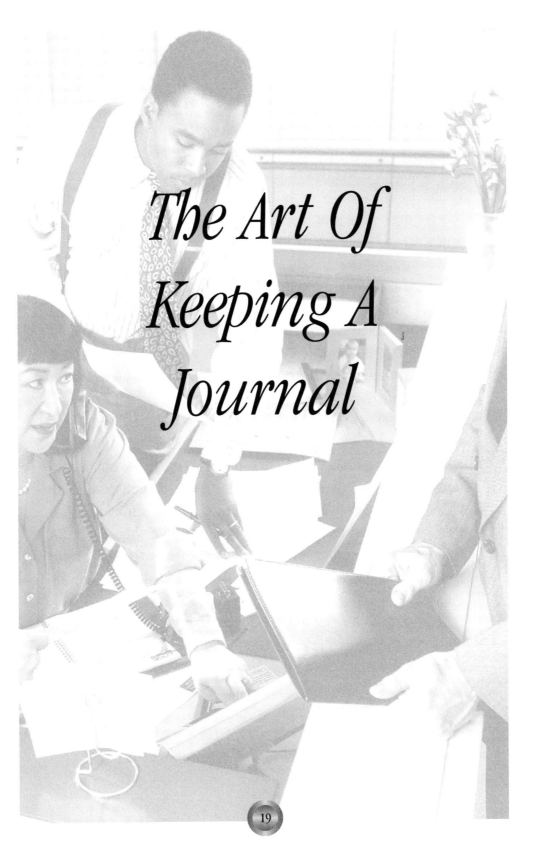

The Art Of Keeping A Journal

The Art of Keeping a Journal

This manual has the potential of changing your life, so you will want to document your progress. Your time and effort, however, will be wasted if you record your thoughts on scraps of paper and eventually lose them. Now is the time to become organized. Since you are organizing your life, why not organize your thoughts about how you will be improving your life?

As you progress through the manual, record your thoughts on loose-leaf paper and keep them in a three-ring binder. The flexibility of a loose-leaf notebook will allow you to add and subtract pages and change the order of your work as you see fit. If you want to get fancy, take a trip to the local book store and find an actual journal containing blank pages. Either way, you will only be investing a few dollars, but the returns will be priceless.

Weight-lifters who are serious about their work regimens often record each exercise such as how many sets they performed and how much weight they lifted. The record-keeping not only keeps track of their progress, but records the results on something tangible, the pages in their journal. By keeping a journal, you will have concrete results of your progress at your fingertips. You can reference your progress and also build momentum from recognition of past successes as you solidify a foundation for life by building nerves of steel.

Take note on how different and energized you feel as you begin to develop nerves of steel and begin living life like it was meant to be lived. You can write down a gambit of material, from what you accomplished during your day to your innermost thoughts and concerns. Keep your journal by your bedside in case you wake up in the middle of the night as a result of a dream or a revelation that popped into your head. Record your experience immediately or it will only be a blurb or will be completely forgotten by morning.

Always keep a small tablet and pen or pencil on hand at all times. Some people even keep a small tape recorder in their pocket, purse, or glove box. As you go through the day, ideas and thoughts that pop into your head can be recorded and referenced later. Many scientists and great thinkers of the world have commented that one of their most useful tools was simply keeping a pencil and paper on hand at all times to record thoughts during the day.

Keeping a journal may not seem important to you because you may not feel your life is worth documenting. However, try keeping a journal for a month or two, and then merely forget about it. Return after several days or weeks and read what you wrote. You will be fascinated about what you were thinking or what you accomplished in the past. You will become addicted to recording your experiences as a way to observe yourself improving your life as you develop nerves of steel.

When historians, anthropologists, sociologists, and other scientists conduct research regarding the past, in many instances, information provided by journals or diaries are the most lucrative sources available. Many accounts of wars, such as the American Civil War, are more vivid and dramatic from diary resources than any textbooks or history books written. The *Diary of Anne Frank* is a classic example.

Henry David Thoreau was one of America's most eloquent writers. Thoreau began recording a personal journal in 1837, when he was only twenty years of age, and he filled over fourteen volumes by the time his life neared its end in 1862. Most of his writings, such as *The Maine Woods*, and *Cape Cod*, are simply a collection of his thoughts and observations. One of his most well-known pieces is *Walden*, a compendium of Thoreau's experiences while he lived by himself in a cabin on the shore of Walden Pond. These writings were, for the most part, journal entries to Thoreau, but have survived as classic collections of stories and have been well-loved by millions of readers.

You will not improve your life in one day for the same reason you will not be completely healthy after one exercise. If you improve only slightly each day, however, your momentum will snowball until you look back several months or years later and shock yourself how far you have come in a certain time period. The classic story of the tortoise and the hare demonstrates the concept of obtaining new skills slowly, but surely.

If you need to diet, it makes more sense to lose a pound a week for 26 weeks rather than trying to lose 26 pounds in a week. Most dieters that crash-diet gain back all the weight they lost and then some. Why? The medical and physical reasons for this dilemma is beyond the scope of this book, but for simplicity's sake just remember that your body cannot take the stress of such a drastic change in a short period of time. Your body will retaliate like a large rubber band fighting to snap back to its original shape after you pull it. Your mind and body are no different.

The process you will be going through while reading this book will be as enjoyable and life-changing as you make it. If you give maximum effort, you will reap maximum rewards. And what better way to relish your accomplishments than by recording your experiences for future enjoyment?

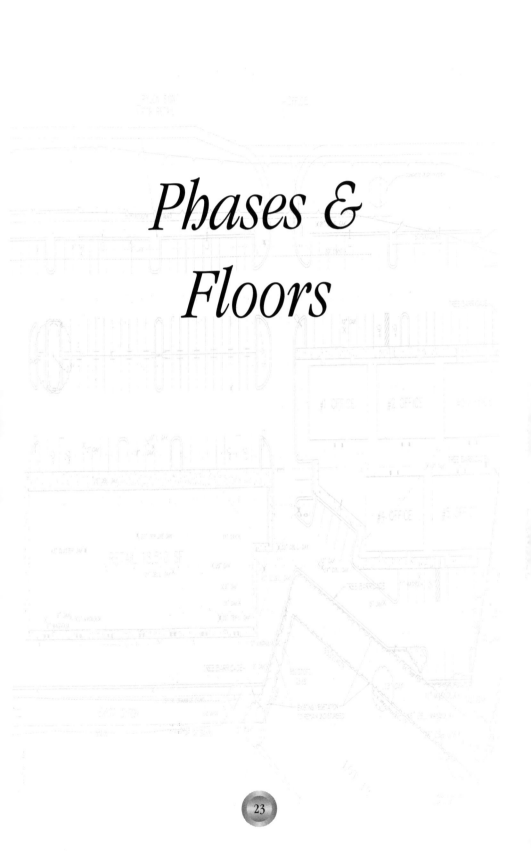

Phases & Floors

PHASE ONE-Plan Your Life (Building A Nerves of Steel Foundation)

Floor One: How To Motivate Yourself Using That Something Inside of You (Identifying What Motivates You)

Floor Two: How To Stop Worrying and Start Gardening (Realizing That "Something" and Developing Proper Focus)

Floor Three: How To Plant Grass Rather Than Pull Weeds (Developing The *Nerves of Steel* Way of Thinking)

Floor Four: How To Get Tougher On Life Instead of Wishing Life Was Easier On You. (Avoiding Self-Pity)

Floor Five: How To Stop, Walk, and then Run In Order to Avoid Coasting (Develop and Stay on Course of Living Life To Its Fullest)

PHASE TWO-Live Your Plan (Finishing Construction)

Floor Six: Don't Be A Feather In The Wind (Live Life In The Zone)

Floor Seven: Beware of The Voice of Judgment (Ridding Yourself of Fear)

Floor Eight: What You Think Is What You Get
   (Develop Thinking Motivators)

The Penthouse Floor: Forgiveness, The Ultimate Strategy
   (How to Forgive)

FLOOR ONE
How To Motivate Yourself Using That Something Inside Of You

"My feets is tired, but my soul is at rest." - **Martin Luther King**, referenced in *"Letter From the Birmingham Jail"* by a 72-year-old woman who walked with him every day during the bus boycott.

Motivate Yourself

All of us are motivated in different ways, but those with nerves of steel are driven by that "something" inside, not by external rewards, such as pats on the back, or verbal praise. People with nerves of steel have tapped the strength inside of them to achieve what they want in their careers (not the same as a job), their relationships, and their lives.

Back when I was a teacher, sometimes I would stay late at school, preparing lessons for the next day. Often, there was nobody left besides me and the janitors, so I was surprised when I heard a knocking at my classroom door one particular night. I looked up and saw Mary, the janitor who cleaned my end of the building.

"I know you do not want to be bothered, but please come and see something," Mary said.

She escorted me into the hall and pointed to the floor, which now had a mirror-like finish.

Mary stood there with a humble smile of satisfaction on her face. I was moved. I had new respect and admiration for her because she was so motivated and excited about her work.

Realize The Difference Between Success And Failure

In 1996, the United States Hockey Team was expected to win a gold medal in the winter Olympics. Their lack of focus, however, was widely publicized and criticized. The team did not win one game.

But the Czech Republic team that same year was very different. Their captain, National Hockey League star Jaromir Jagr, wore number 68 because 1968 was the year of the Soviet occupation of Czechoslovakia. Guess who the Czech Republic played for the chance to advance their dreams and achieve the gold medal? Russia.

According to Jagr, before the deciding game, everyone in the locker room was thinking about the Russian occupation of Czechoslovakia. The team dedicated the game to their families and to other families who lost loved ones because of the occupation. The Czech Republic team brought home the gold medal.

Do you think the Czechs were nervous on the ice? Sure. But on that night, the Czechs used nerves of steel to turn their butterflies into positive adrenaline. The Czechs showed more determination than any other hockey team. Each and every team member knew what it would take to achieve victory, gave 110 percent, and made their dream come true.

What is your "68," or your main purpose for living? If you have no direction in life, you are merely wandering around like a ship lost at sea with no rudder or steersman.

I went to law school with a gentleman whose mother was suffering from cancer. She always wished that she would be around when her son graduated. Two weeks after she wrote the check for the last installment of her son's law school tuition, she passed away.

Values tend to be picked out in a haphazard, piecemeal fashion from friends, parents, the media, teachers, popular heroes, and clergy, in that order.[1]

Baumeister (1991) felt if we satisfy four important needs, we can add meaning to our life. The needs are to have purpose, which would include devising goals; the need to have value, which would include our morals and ethics; the need to feel effective, capable, or in control, and the need for self-worth, or finding a basis for feeling positive about our lives.[2]

Make Your Dreams Come True

You have the ability right now to make your dreams come true. The first step is to identify your dreams and motivating forces, and then develop the ability to focus and keep your dreams in your foreground.

Two types of motivation exist: intrinsic and extrinsic. Intrinsic motivation is far more essential to develop nerves of steel, but extrinsic motivation is important as well, because it is often the root for feeling overwhelmed and losing focus.

Bandura (1986) concluded that human behavior is largely self-regulated, and that intrinsic reinforcement may be better than external reinforcement.

Extrinsic motivational forces are factors outside of your control, the carrot in front of the horse. If the boss of a pharmaceutical firm tells a researcher he will be given a raise if he is successful in developing a new medication, the researcher will certainly be motivated. This sort of motivation, however, forces the employee to find the solution, which may also cause undue nervousness or stress. The employee may feel overwhelmed and perhaps lose motivation and focus.

Two of the most common extrinsic rewards are financial rewards and the need to have approval of your actions by others. The nervousness stems from a belief that a person must have these rewards or else personal well-being is threatened. Therefore, it is much harder to develop nerves of steel if you are motivated by extrinsic rewards. You may start out feeling motivated after being told you would receive a raise or a bonus if you are successful, but eventually, you will feel bribed or controlled by the extrinsic rewards. Such feelings may even be subconscious, meaning the feelings would not be obvious to you at first.

Extrinsic rewards, in some circumstances, may turn fun into work, lower our motivation to perform the work, and reduce the amount of innovativeness or thinking we do concerning the work at hand, which would make our behavior more automated and stereotypical.[3]

Economist W. Edwards Deming told the story in many of his seminars about the bellboy who went out of his way to help a crippled gentleman get his bags from his room into the taxi. The bellboy took pride in providing the gentleman with extra special care but was crushed when the gentleman handed him a tip.

Do It Now

Have you ever procrastinated? We all are guilty. Have you ever wondered why you seem to procrastinate? Do you want to move your life up to the next level, whether it be at your job or your personal relationships, or some other area, but you never seem to get that positive momentum started? Have you ever said to yourself for years you were going to start your own business but never went any further than just wondering what it would be like to be your

29

own boss? Have you ever made New Year's resolutions that lasted about six days, six hours, or even six minutes? Is your garage or attic still a mess after years of saying you were going to finally do some serious housecleaning.

If you consider the only reward for cleaning your garage or attic to be that your spouse will stop nagging you, that is an extrinsic reward. However, if you consider the sense of achievement and personal satisfaction you will feel after you clean the attic or garage, that is an intrinsic reward.

Intrinsic rewards are based on passion and internal desire. The first key to developing nerves of steel is to identify what intrinsically motivates you and to keep those factors continuously in front of you. When you are intrinsically motivated, you perform because you love the challenge or enjoy the activity. Even work can be rewarding if you are doing the job because you love it, not because you have to do it. Mary, the cleaning woman at the school, was probably not extrinsically rewarded based upon what she was probably being paid, but she was definitely intrinsically motivated because she took so much pride in her nice, shiny floors.

Fair and Lynette (1992) found that intrinsically motivated people perform better than extrinsically motivated people. Their study credits positive affirmations from inside as a factor in increasing motivation. External rewards and punishment were attributed to decreasing motivation.

The key is for you to motivate yourself from inside regarding your actions because you will never perform to the best of your ability by virtue of only outside motivational factors, such as pay increases, expected approval from others, or disciplinary threats.

Observations of high achievers in business and sports have shown that people perform best when they are motivated by interest, satisfaction, challenge, and love of their work. Motivation by external pressure rarely motivates an individual enough to perform to the best of his or her ability.

Joel Steed was a perennial all-pro with the Pittsburgh Steelers of the National Football League. He arrived in Pittsburgh via the third round of the 1992 draft. When he came to the team from the University of Colorado, he was good, but not good enough to make an impact right away.

In fact, he was not even good enough to dress for games. I sat down with him when he first came to Pittsburgh. I instructed Joel to write down on a card what was important to him and to place the card in a place where he could always be reminded how he felt.

Our initial focus was not to spend any mental energy on what was happening to him, but to concentrate on getting better at the game of football. If, everyday, he got just a little bit better, eventually he would become a successful NFL player. We entitled the card "Getting Better Vision" and he viewed it daily. The card focused on four topics: Getting Better Every Day, Helping Someone Else With An Encouraging Word, Having Fun, and Celebrating Life With Family. At the end of each day, he would call up a memory of something that happened that day that fit in with one of these values. He would also frequently call my voice mail service and leave messages about the vision he had of becoming a better player every day.

The coaches saw improvement every week in his playing. In time, Joel was good enough to start, and he was excellent on the field, but he kept working even harder on himself. Joel became mentally stronger by reacting to cues and learning tendencies of others. At this point, Joel was working harder on himself than on football. When his next contract was negotiated, he signed one of the largest contracts ever awarded to a defensive lineman by the Pittsburgh Steelers.

If you work hard in your occupation, you will develop a career. If you work hard on yourself, you will strike a fortune. You must realize the importance of your intrinsic motivators and concentrate on them as much or more than you concentrate on outside motivators. Examples of your intrinsic motivators may be having fun in life, to be a better parent, or to find a job you love. We will demonstrate tools which have the potential of allowing you to achieve all of the above if you apply yourself. In Joel Steed's case, his motivating factors were to grow to be a better person and to devote more time to his family.

Work At A Job You Love, or Love The Job You Have

Who is not busy in today's workplace? Everyone complains about being overwhelmed or stressed. In the health care profession, nurses state they are more overwhelmed than ever before. Why do most doctors and nurses enter the health care field? An extrinsic motivator may be money or prestige. An intrinsic motivator may be to help and care for people. Health care-related companies in this country, however, must now concentrate heavily on health insurance requirements, quotas, and liability suits in order to stay in business.

Doctors and nurses are forced to do more paperwork and worry more about forms, charts and documents than about patients' health concerns. By filling out the forms and charts, a nurse or doctor is still being paid, so their extrinsic motivators are being satisfied. But are their intrinsic motivators of helping and caring for the sick being satisfied? Perhaps not. Maybe the lack of intrinsic motivators is more the problem than the pressure the job creates.

By re-addressing each time-consuming task, no matter how meaningless it may seem, as actually contributing to care for the sick, health-care professionals may find a new attitude in doing their jobs. Any job can be rewarding provided you find the intrinsic reasons you are performing your job and concentrate on the intrinsic rewards you receive while working.

Cognitive dissonance is a term defined as a person's behavior when it is out of line with his or her intrinsic needs which causes one to be mentally uncomfortable. The mind becomes confused, producing brain waves and unpleasantness similar to hearing a seven-year-old bang on a bunch of piano keys in no musical order. When you identify your intrinsic needs, you tend to act in ways that are aligned with those needs. When your behavior is not aligned with your intrinsic needs, you experience cognitive dissonance.

John Majors was both a college football player and a college football coach. During his tenure at the University of Pittsburgh, Majors coached a Heisman Trophy winner, Tony Dorsett, who later played professionally with the Dallas Cowboys. Both Majors and Dorsett knew their intrinsic needs and used them to create life-fulfilling destinies.

Majors earned all-American honors as a tailback at the University of Tennessee in his collegiate days. In 1956, he finished second in the Heisman Trophy balloting, behind Notre Dame's Paul Hornung. In 1972, he arrived at the University of Pittsburgh as its twenty-sixth head coach in the school's history. He turned around a once-proud but downtrodden program into a national powerhouse and with the help of Tony Dorsett, led the Panthers to a national championship in 1976.

Tony Dorsett was constantly told growing up that he was too

small to play football. In order to weigh enough to qualify for the minimum weight as a pee wee football player, Dorsett commented that he put rocks in his pocket before he got on the scale. During his playing days at the University of Pittsburgh, he shattered not only the school's rushing record but the all-time Division I college rushing record at that time by running for 6,082 yards.

Dorsett was the only player in the history of the game of football to win an NCAA Division One college football national championship, a Heisman Trophy, and an NFL Super Bowl Championship, and also to be inducted into the College and Professional Football Halls of Fame. At a celebration of the anniversary of Pittsburgh's national championship, Dorsett commented on how well Majors treated his players.

"Coach Majors was an excellent communicator and he related well to the players," Dorsett said. "He treated us not like kids, but like young men."

Majors always believed in treating his players like men. He recollected, when the team was playing for the national championship, that he did not place a curfew on his players earlier in the game-week because he had thought they earned the right to be treated like men, not like children. He felt the players would be motivated to police themselves due to their intrinsic values, which were to experience the joy inside of each of them by helping their team win a national championship.

If anyone was a good judge of motivating people, it would be John Majors, so I asked Coach Majors who was the best motivator he ever knew. He responded by saying Bill McCartney, former head coach at the University of Colorado. Majors said that McCartney would ask every athlete what motivated him and how he was going to meet that motivational need. McCartney told Majors that once an athlete identified what motivated him, then McCartney would teach the athlete to align his behavior in order to achieve his intrinsic needs.

Due to being intrinsically motivated by such a strong belief in his faith, McCartney quit coaching Division I college football to pursue other paths including writing books and the founding of the Promise Keepers Christian fellowship.

An important key to eternal happiness is to develop a career doing what you love rather than to concentrate on doing a job you feel will pay you enough money. Being unhappy at work can kill you. You can endanger your health and welfare by working a job which makes you unhappy.

The best way to eliminate pressure on the job is to work in a field you love doing what you would do if money was not a concern. It is not recommended to immediately quit your job just because you feel unhappy, but you can eliminate some unhappiness from a job you feel you hate while you draw up an action plan to design a career in a capacity you feel destined toward. If you are not satisfied with your current occupation, take two steps forward in eliminating unhappiness on your job.

1) Decide what intrinsically motivates you and link those feelings somehow with your current job.

2) Decide what your dream job would be and take steps toward achieving that goal.

(More detail will be discussed in later chapters concerning these two points.)

Gain Support For Your Cause

Do not be afraid to share your beliefs or new concerns with other people, especially spouses, close family, or anybody you feel has a vested interest in your well-being. Sharing your beliefs with other people reinforces your drive toward developing nerves of steel.

Many organizations world-wide would love to have the success realized by Alcoholics Anonymous or AA. Despite an absence of buildings or formal structures, AA has a phenomenal record of success. During meetings, which are open to virtually anyone looking for help, people in attendance have a chance to share their experiences with alcohol, solutions, the advantages and life-changing aspects of living sober, or simply something they want to get off their chest. During most AA meetings, people pour their feelings out like water in a bucket with holes punctured in the bottom.

One key to the success of AA is the participants' opportunity to share personal feelings with other people, especially their motivation for staying sober. The concept absolutely works for a great deal of its participants in allowing members to focus on the goal of not drinking. Alcoholics know they cannot change the fact they are alcoholics, but by sharing their experiences with others, they have the ability to conquer the strangle-hold alcoholism forces on them through the catharsis of accepting themselves as alcoholics and the fellowship granted among all in attendance.

They become the best they can be by sharing one of their sayings with themselves and others. "I'm not okay, and you're not okay, but that's okay."

Other AA mottos can be frequently seen on car bumper stickers and include sayings such as *One Day At A Time* and *Believe in Miracles*.

PROFILE OF STEEL

Sandra worked in a low-paying, fast-paced environment as a secretary for an investment brokerage firm in Seattle, Washington. She was married and had one daughter and was also taking care of her live-in mother. As if her life was not stressful enough, Sandra's husband picked up and left her for a younger woman who worked at his place of employment. She was now burdened with the sole responsibility of taking care of her daughter and her mother.

During one of her workdays, Sandra was thinking out loud and simply said to her boss, "I would like to work in the same capacity as you some day."

Her boss answered back with the snide remark, "You could never do what I do!" He might as well have stabbed Sandra in the heart, because she was so deeply hurt by his remark.

That night, Sandra was so angry, she could not sleep. In the midst of her sleeplessness, her anger proved to be beneficial in this instance. She was suddenly aroused with the revelation that she had been dedicating her entire life to the benefit of other people: her former husband, her daughter, her mother, and even her boss, leaving no nurturing for herself. Things would soon change. Sandra intrinsically motivated herself by wanting to be independent as well as to live a life she was proud of and to have her daughter witness this transformation of her becoming a fully-alive woman.

Sandra went back to school and received a degree. She then attended some investment classes that allowed her to receive a brokerage license shortly thereafter. She now works for a more prestigious firm in the same industry as her former employer and makes twice as much as her former boss.

How do you react to your revelations, by taking action or letting them evaporate?

DIALOGUE OF STEEL

If Sandra would have listened to her self-defeating, mushy dialogue for the rest of her life, she would still be nowhere, living an uneventful, hapless life as a miserable office assistant. Instead, she used her anger as a motivating force and fought back her self-dialogue of mush by attacking with a dialogue of steel until she created a happy and meaningful life for herself.

Sandra's Dialogue of Mush: Not only does my boss think I'm a loser, but even my husband thinks I am such a loser that he leaves me for good.

Sandra's Dialogue of Steel: Their opinion does not equal my opinion.

Sandra's DOM: I have never done anything meaningful before.

Sandra's DOS: That does not mean I can't do anything meaningful now; I can change.

Sandra's DOM: I have always been this way.

Sandra's DOS: "Always" does not mean "Always will be." Instead of worrying about pleasing everybody else, I will now concentrate on being fully alive.

Sandra's DOM: I can't keep up this positive attitude day after day.

Sandra's DOS: I can stay on my newly created path of destiny by taking one day at a time.

It is possible for you to get the upper hand on the destructive forces of your mind by initiating and continuing similar Nerves of Steel Dialogue with yourself on a daily basis.

NUTS AND BOLTS FROM NERVES OF STEEL-FLOOR ONE
How To Motivate Yourself Using That Something Inside of You

Realize the importance of motivating yourself. There IS a difference between success and failure. If you are not living your life with a major purpose in mind, you are not living life. You are meandering through life and merely going through the motions. Your grandparents may have called this haphazard, irresponsible lifestyle "living from post to pole."

If you have no plan for your life, how do you know if you are succeeding or failing? One of the most important aspects of developing nerves of steel is to find your major purpose on this earth and then to develop a road map that leads you to your destiny. By mapping out your major purpose, you are turning your wishes into dreams. You can make your dreams come true if you find your intrinsic motivators and use them to your advantage.

During your journey, you will be forced to dodge obstructions such as procrastination that will attempt to hold you back every step of your journey. More will be discussed later about how to combat these negative forces.

Since most people spend more time at their jobs and with their co-workers than they spend with their family each week, why not work at a career you love, instead of forcing yourself to go to a job every day that you hate? Ask yourself the question, "If money was no object, what would I want to do for the rest of my life?"

Inform your family and friends that you are now in pursuit of your dream job. Oftentimes, you will magically receive help from these sources that you did not anticipate. Gain support for your cause or your newly-found purpose in life.

Motivate yourself every day, just as you would take a bath or a shower, or put on makeup, or go to the gym. When your mind tries to sabotage you, which is prevalent any time you attempt to initiate new, positive changes in your life, argue with your mind and sway those negative thoughts toward positive ones, almost as if you are debating with yourself. Your mind will automatically take the side of the negative debater, so combat it by taking the side of the positive debater. Observe how successful you get at driving the negative forces from your self-dialogue.

seed which must be given hope, vision, nurturing, and fertile ground in order to germinate. There is no doubt Bruce Lee developed a phenomenal focus-ability from the substantial martial arts training he endured. Another factor contributing to Lee's ability to define a goal and focus on the outcome without waiver was his study of philosophy at the University of Washington in Seattle.

Because of his extensive training in the complementary areas of martial arts as well as philosophy, Lee may have gained an edge in focusing on goals compared to the average person, but focusing skills can be developed by virtually any person of normal mind.

Actress Sally Fields once said that, immediately after she was born, the doctor should not have told her mother, "Congratulations, you have just delivered a baby girl!" but instead should have said, "Congratulations, you have just delivered an actress."

Fields played magnificent roles in many movies including *Forest Gump, Places of the Heart, Norma Rae, and Cybil.* She said she never wanted to be a doctor, an attorney, or an anthropologist while growing up, but could see herself playing those parts as an actress. She realized that "something" was inside of her as a teenager when she performed in the school play, and acted on that passion which enabled her to create her own destiny. Is Sally Fields different than anyone else? Absolutely not.

Former U.S. Chief of Staff and current Secretary of State Colin Powell was a below average student. He struggled in high school and college. One day, however, he watched the ROTC class march by at Brooklyn College and that "something" inside of him came alive. He instantly realized he wanted to become a soldier. Although his grades were not good at that time, he excelled in

ROTC because he discovered that seed inside of himself and had the discipline and courage to nurture it. After he entered the military and started climbing up the ladder, he turned down desk jobs along the way in order to remain where he felt he belonged in the field. For his dedication and hard work, Powell was appointed United States Secretary of State, under President George W. Bush.

Calvin Kline, the famous clothes designer, would watch other children playing outside, but he always chose to stay inside and draw clothing. He did not know where his desires came from at that time, but he realized his purpose in life at an early age and acted on it. He has drawn himself into a multi-million dollar empire.

Michael Moschen is one of the world's greatest jugglers and has performed to sell-out audiences around the world. He started juggling when he was twelve years old.

"Juggling was strange, interesting, and difficult," Moschen said, "but I liked it."

He remembers the day as a young boy when he was riding the bus back home from his job of picking tobacco and he glanced down at his weather-beaten hands. He realized at that instant that his hands were meant for finer things. He discovered his destiny and became a successful juggler.

Michael Romano is one of America's top-ten chefs according to *Food & Wine Magazine*. When he was a child, Michael would visit his aunts and uncles after church. He would watch them prepare the food so intensely that he finally yearned to be in the middle of the preparation. He began by making the handmade pastas. He was most impressed by the commitment to dedicate an entire day to prepare a complex meal, just so it could be successfully presented. He knew at that time he wanted to spend the rest of his life engaging in day-long meal preparation.

"I sometimes feel guilty because I was just going with the flow of what life had to offer. It felt almost out of my hands, like a voice was telling me that this is where I need to be now and let me see what I could find out," Romano said. "Wonderful opportunities just seemed to present themselves to me at every point."

Do we always know what our seed is? No. Do we always get our seed right? No. Often because we want to tell the seed what kind of plant it is, instead of letting the seed grow up into the plant it is pre-determined to be. We do not want to listen or surrender to our calling in life.

T.S. Elliot summed up the idea concerning the seed inside of our garden that is just waiting to be watered and cared for until it blooms and blossoms when he said, *"I said to my soul be still and wait without hope. For hope will be hope for the wrong thing."*

Unearth Your Seed Of Destiny

You are influenced every day by other people, your parents, your siblings, your spouse or significant other, your children, your friends, your co-workers, your clergy, your teacher or mentor, or simply by your surroundings. None of them can tell you what your seed of destiny is; only you can determine how to spend the rest of your life. Once you find your seed of destiny, the planting and growing instructions will appear to you. If you have the courage to become a successful gardener by becoming a champion toward your seed of destiny, rather than trying to re-invent your seed, you will experience bliss.

Super Bowl XXXIV was played on January 30, 2000, in Atlanta, Georgia, between the St. Louis Rams and the Tennessee Titans.

Rams quarterback Kurt Warner was a prime example of a person going for his dreams at all costs. After he finished his college playing career, he was unable to successfully earn a position with a team in the National Football League. The Green Bay Packers was one such team that cast him aside. He chose to play in the low-paying Arena Football League in the evenings and stock shelves with canned goods at a local supermarket during the day. He then played in the European Football League and was finally noticed again by the NFL, but this time around, the story would have a different outcome.

The Los Angeles Rams signed Warner as a backup to starting quarterback Trent Green. When Green was hurt before the season started, Warner's number was called. He worked his entire life for this chance. Since he never faltered in preparing to be a starting quarterback in the NFL, when his day came, he made the most of his chance. Warner earned NFL Most Valuable Player Honors. He led the Rams to the Super Bowl and capped off his dream season in style by throwing the winning touchdown with less than two minutes left in the game.

Following the game, ESPN broadcaster Mike Terico interviewed Warner and asked him how he found the guts and courage to keep following his dream. Warner pointed out that he never let go of his dream, kept constant focus, and worked hard. Eventually his dreams came true.

Every life lived to its fullest is a masterpiece, every life lived aimlessly is a tragedy. How immense could your life be if you surrendered to your seed of destiny and nurtured its growth? If you can learn to focus your energy on extending your seed out into the world and up to the heavens, you will truly become a champion.

I was not a particularly strong high school student, but it was even more difficult on me because I followed a sister who was. When I would bring my report card home, my father would look at it and say, "You should be ashamed of this report card, your sister's report card does not have one "B" on it. I would say, "Neither does mine," which was true because I would earn nothing above a "C."

My sister was senior class president, gridiron queen, valedictorian, and even Mary in the church Christmas play. I was expected to follow in her footsteps. My mother would keep saying to me, "You can do it whenever you find what it is you're supposed to be doing."

She was right. I loved studying behavior right up to the time I got my doctorate. After I was awarded my diploma, I took her out to dinner and told her, "I appreciate you encouraging me because it helped me get to where I am."

She sat quiet for a minute, and then said, "Kevin, I never thought you were going to amount to anything, but I didn't know what else to say, so you shocked me."

Oh, well, it still worked. I found my seed and nurtured it with her help and I shocked myself and her by doing so.

You have a plan buried inside the garden of your mind. The "truth," however, is that your plan is not always easy to find. You may have to struggle to find it. If you have the courage to tackle those struggles, observe what makes you come alive. When you find the "truth" or your purpose in life, you will shock yourself by realizing how much more wonderful your world will become.

Regarding each person's purpose in life, Henry David Thoreau wrote:

A just man's purpose cannot be split on any Grampus or

material rock, but itself will split rocks till it succeeds.[1]

The truth, however, can also be painful, because the truth often means battling with your ego. The death of the small ego, however, allows the larger self to emerge. Your ego may want you to be something other than what your seed wants you to be. Your ego may want you to be in a position of power, while your seed may be designed for you to be in a position of service.

Your ego may not realize that a position of service can be a position of power. Your ego may say we have to satisfy friends and family to be what they think we should be. But your seed knows best. It says you will find peace wrapped inside of it when you surrender to the internal calling.

Realize Your Garden May Become Trampled And Weed-Infested

One reason many people never germinate their seed is their belief that the internal seed of destiny is an illusion or a myth. Many formal school curriculum help reinforce this belief. Although schools are attempting to improve over time, cultivating our internal seeds is not usually part of most schools' curriculum. Schools with outdated curriculum force students to become proficient in rote memorization. If a student is unable to learn within this centuries-old system of education, he or she is negatively labeled.

Parents can add to the negative reinforcement by insisting that the success of their children also depends on such criteria, and seeking therapists to help destroys the labels that have been crystallized in the children's minds if they do not conform. In many instances, any hope that the individual has left in believing in himself or herself is destroyed, which also tramples their inner seed that was planted inside of their minds.

As mentioned in the introduction, Thomas Edison was a failure in a formal school setting. Pulitzer Prize winning writer Ellen Glasgow thought school was intolerable. Pearl S. Buck and Susan B. Anthony all disliked school. Albert Einstein said that he preferred all sorts of punishment over the endurance of rote memorization that was emphasized in the schools of his day and is still emphasized today in most schools. William Faulkner and F. Scott Fitzgerald failed courses in college. H.G. Wells was slated for retail trade by his counselors and was forced into literature after breaking his leg.

Gisele Ben-Dor is one of the most exciting musical conductors today. She was born in Uruguay of Polish parents and graduated from the Rubin Academy of Music in Tel-Aviv, and the Yale School of Music. She recalls, however, that some teachers told her she would never be a conductor. Certain teachers were even ashamed of admitting she was their student. Ben-Dor said that, in most areas of her life, she is usually conservative, but she knew that her seed of destiny was musical conducting. She took the mentality of following her instincts, taking some risks, and seeing what happens. What happened was a standing ovation in her debut with the New York Philharmonic.

Virginia Johnson is a gifted ballerina who maintains a strong work ethic. She was the first African-American to dance the ballet entitled *Giselle* with the Royal Ballet in London. She studied ballet during her entire academic life, but her dance teachers advised her to move on to modern dance or maybe jazz. They felt she could not succeed in ballet as an African-American. Johnson remembers the feeling of betrayal bestowed upon her at that time due to all the support they had given her during her years of dance classes. She did not trample down her seed of destiny, however, and gardened harder than ever until she became one of the world's greatest ballerinas.

Every one of these maximum achievers were provided evidence at an earlier age that, since they could not master a particular educational system, they were intellectual failures. People who refuse to live lives of desperation are usually people who recognize their seed of destiny, become excellent gardeners through hard and smart work, and realize their dreams first hand. People who refuse to acknowledge their destiny and then take action based on their findings but still think someday things may change will never nurture their seeds of destiny to fruition.

School instruction is important, but success or failure in school can only be considered a variable, not a constant. When a student is failing, a good teacher should be able to see the angel in the malady and should safeguard a failing student's seed of destiny by attempting to find out what that particular student is interested in learning.

Parents should be the main influence on this earth regarding their children's lives and should never force a child to be something he or she is not destined to be. If parents do not attempt to nurture their child's seed of destiny, they are doing a great disservice toward their children. Sometimes, parents even attempt to live their lives through their children, by trying to pull seeds they found inside themselves and transplanting them in their children's minds. If the child submits to this transplanting and those seeds do not match, the child is submitting to faulty programming. A faulty computer program can wreak havoc. A child's mind is no different. There is a saying among computer programmers that states, "Garbage in, Garbage out."

If you are a parent and want to realize your own seed of destiny, do not force your calling on your offspring, but rather unearth your own seed and begin to become a master gardener of your own dreams and desires, and help your family members achieve their own dreams and goals. If you did not learn this concept from your parents, it is simply time to become your own great parent.

"The Gods Have Become Diseases"

These above words by Carl Jung are sill alive and well today. But when these gods (no relation to God in heaven) are done working on you, often it is you who is diseased. If you are living a life dictated by necessity rather than influenced by your internal seed of destiny, disease can become a by-product of your unhealthy life. Many people say they have to continue making a living rather than to follow their destiny in order to make enough money to survive. Such an attitude turns a living into a job, rather than a job into a living.

If you are concerned with the necessity of making a living, consider this fact. Somewhere, there are people making money, maybe even very good money, performing the same activities that you would love to be doing. They just figured out how to do it. Consider following their example and maybe even obtaining advice from them to be used for future reference in your quest for your destiny.

Writer George Sheehan was a physician before he realized his seed of destiny.

"When I did what they wanted me to do, I used to count my money," Sheehan said. "But now that I am doing what I want to do, I weigh it."

Sheehan held an image in his mind of being told when to be at work, when to leave, and what to do. He could have done this his entire life and then be presented with a watch upon retirement.

Once he realized the trap he was falling into, he quivered.

Fiction author Michael Creighton worked his way through medical school by writing books. By the time he graduated medical school, he was already established enough as a writer that he decided to continue using a pen rather than a stethoscope. He found an excellent way of utilizing his formal medical training in the process by writing medical-related books, or using medical information within his well-crafted stories.

By trusting your instinct, you will be trusting your seed, you will be placing courage in yourself, not in the "gods" or the authorities who convinced you of something else. The best authority on earth you can consult is yourself. Listen, trust, and act. Only then will you be living with nerves of steel.

If you become worried about the decisions you may have to make in the future, ask yourself, "What is the worst thing that can possibly happen to me?" Once you focus on that question and its eventual outcomes, usually you realize that perhaps the consequences will not be as bad as you first thought.

The Courage To Start New Careers

Nikos Kazantzakis, famous author of *Zorba The Greek*, was sitting at the base of a tree one day when he spotted a cocoon breaking open. He was fascinated with the beauty of the manifestation he was witnessing and decided he would help this butterfly emerge into the world. He breathed his warm breath upon the cocoon hoping he would hurry the process. His breath, however, was incapable of achieving what only the natural heat of the sun could accomplish. The butterfly wings did not dry properly, got stuck together, causing the butterfly to die in the hands of the author.

In your life, you are often given cocoons. Each of these cocoons gives rise to your next endeavor and without the struggle of breaking free of your cocoon and the drying of your wings by the sun, you may not be strong enough to enter into the next endeavor. That next endeavor may be necessary in order to fulfill your calling in life.

When I was in college for four years, I worked in a grocery store stocking shelves and carrying customers' bags. I learned more in that store than I did in my formal classes. I entered the teaching profession and taught at the high school level. I eventually moved into the middle school level. I obtained the needed education and broke free from my cocoon and became a therapist. Finally, I became a lecturer and an author. Every step was necessary along the way to advance to the next world that was calling.

You can cope with pressure either by approaching it or avoiding it. The first method reduces discomfort while the second method increases the chances to cope. Both methods may be appropriate depending on the situation. By reducing the discomfort from just following the status quo, you may be prolonging your misery. If you approach the situations you find to be troublesome, such as a bad relationship or a job you hate, you will be taking positive action toward a problem that may be sabotaging your life.

I ran into a woman in Williamsport, Pennsylvania, who told me she was suffering from cancer. She enjoyed attending a cancer victim support group, but always found herself talking about how much stress her divorce thrust on her life.

Other group members urged her to take some time off and do something she always dreamed of doing. She took their advice. She traveled to Tibet and rode in a mountain bike tour for a month.

When she returned, she was shocked to find out that not only did her stress about her divorce leave her, but the cancer was nowhere to be found either.

PROFILE OF STEEL

Mindy attended the University of Pittsburgh and was also a member of the diving team. After college, she found a job as a mental health administrator and performed well for seven years. One day Mindy realized she had become bored with her present job. This feeling sparked some inner urges inside Mindy that made her realize what she really wanted to do, which was to dive at the competitive level once again as well as become a counselor and a writer.

Mindy committed herself to follow her instincts and took the big dive into that pool of uncertainty. She now conducts workshops for children coping with divorced parents instead of working at a job that bored her. She also has entered the competitive diving arena once again, but this time she is not worrying if she wins or loses at diving competitions, because in her mind, she has already won the ultimate prize.

Some people thought she was crazy but maybe she thinks those people are too sane. What do you think?

DIALOGUE OF STEEL

If Mindy would have continued down the same path of boredom for the rest of her life, she may have been the patient in counseling, instead of being the person who followed her dreams and became a counselor herself. Mindy used her dialogue of steel to jump off the diving board into the pool of a happy life rather than to allow her dialogue of mush to force her to hang onto the diving board ladder of boredom.

*Mindy's **Dialogue of Mush**: Even though I feel lifeless in this job, I have to keep working here because I feel it is the responsible thing to do.*
*Mindy's **Dialogue of Steel**: Maybe I feel lifeless in this job for a reason. Maybe it is my instinct to take another direction and my lifelessness is a result of not listening.*
*Mindy's **DOM**: But what if I fail?*
*Mindy's **DOS**: Is it better to succeed at trying something new that does not work out, or to fail at not trying something new, and remain lifeless for my entire life?*
*Mindy's **DOM**: But I do not know what to do or where to start.*
*Mindy's **DOS**: I will start from right where I am right now by writing down the first steps to take and will begin taking those steps tomorrow morning.*

It is possible for you to choose the right path by diving into life, instead of drowning in sorrow and self-pity near the end of your life because you wished you had taken that path before it was too late.

NUTS AND BOLTS FROM NERVES OF STEEL - FLOOR TWO
How To Stop Worrying and Start Gardening

Have you ever wished you were working in a different occupation? Did you ever wonder why you keep torturing yourself if you are currently working in a job you hate? If your inner voice is telling you that you hate your job, you can use the same inner voice to help you find your seed or your purpose in life. You will find it beneficial to also help other people achieve their dreams or purpose in life. By helping other people, you will be shocked at how many doors will mysteriously open which will lead you down your own path as a result.

Where you are and what you are doing at this very moment is a direct result of every decision you made in your life up to this point. Every action you ever took was either a learning experience or a necessity that allowed you to get to where you now stand. If you hate where you are, it may be because you made some bad choices in the past; maybe you were not even aware of some of those choices. You may also be living a meaningless life because you did not learn enough from your mistakes in the past and you also may have made the same mistakes over and over.

FLOOR THREE
How To Plant Grass Rather Than Pull Weeds

"I kissed my first woman and smoked my first cigar on the same day. I have never had time for tobacco since."
Arturo Toscanini

Whenever you get discouraged, do you feel like quitting or giving up, especially when you seem to be putting forth large amounts of time, energy, and resources, but your efforts do not seem to be paying off? This is the precise time when you need to keep planting grass.

One day I called a lawn care service to treat my lawn because it was in poor shape. They arrived the next day, took one look at the lawn, and told me there was nothing they could do because the lawn was beyond help. They rejected my business. I have been rejected before, but never by a lawn care service. I thought this was an all-time low for sure.

So I walked over to my neighbor's house and told him what had happened between myself and the lawn service. I figured I might be able to seek some advice from him concerning bringing my lawn back to life. He stated that he was not sure he could help me but did offer me one piece of advice. He said to keep planting grass, don't pull any weeds, and be patient. I followed his advice and, after a few years, I have a lawn nicer than I could ever imagine in the past.

The Need For A Winning System

Do not focus on your results as much as on the joy of a winning process. Just keep planting grass and have patience. Good things will eventually happen. They must. Develop a winning system. Work your system. The results will seem to appear like magic. Some results may take longer than expected, but use your nerves of steel and have patience.

Your system should avoid the trap of trying to be right or perfect every time, because then your actions may become boring. Current buzzwords in today's business world include phrases such as "quality is job one," and "doing it right the first time." Quality is an important attribute to any task, but acting like a zombie is not. You must go one step further. You must not only focus on quality and perfection, but you should be able to have fun doing it, or what is the use of doing it at all?

Would you ever go out to dinner and a symphony and comment that you had an outstanding evening because it conformed perfectly to your expectations? Quality and perfection should be automatically expected. If you feel blown away by the experience, you had an outstanding evening. If you strive to give extra effort in your career, your relationships, and your life, you are successfully working a system.

You have the ability to help yourself. Who better to address your future than yourself? People have been helping themselves since time began. Scogin, Bynum, Stevens, and Calhoon (1990) conducted an analysis of 40 well-designed studies of self-help treatments and concluded that self-help is clearly more effective than no treatment, and, in many cases, as effective as treatment administered by a therapist.

You must take responsibility for helping yourself. You are solely responsible for where you are in life right now, and where you are going in the future.

Consistency

Few franchises have enjoyed the success of McDonald's restaurants. One cannot count the number of hamburgers they have sold to date. In the Woody Allen movie Sleeper, when he appears in the future, Woody passes by a McDonald's restaurant and the count of hamburgers served is in the billions. McDonald's has now approached that number of hamburgers sold. What is their reason for success?

The answer is simple: consistency. McDonald's is not interested in making the best hamburger; they are only interested in making the same hamburger, every time, no matter where the hamburger is served, from Peoria to Paris. McDonald's has achieved this feat since the inception of its winning system, even with the use of the vast number of employees who have worked in McDonalds's restaurants all over the world since its inception. How did they manage that? By instituting a precise, step-by-step process that was concrete enough that one-in-eight Americans have worked for a McDonald's at one time or another and all have learned the same winning system.

Larry Bird only wanted to be the same player each and every night, one that gives his all. As a result, he became a great player in the NBA.

When Mother Theresa was alive, she told herself she would care for the sick and the poor each day the same way, no matter what afflictions she witnessed.

Ken Griffey, Jr., is consistently one of the best hitters in baseball every year. He tells himself the same thing when he is batting regardless of who the pitcher is, *"See the ball, hit the ball."*

All these people and most everyone who is successful, whether it be in sports, business, charity work, or any vocation, are successful because they have developed a winning system for themselves and they follow their system to a tee. Psychologist Albert Ellis describes this notion best in his well-known *ABC Model of Rational Thinking*. In Ellis' model, "A" stands for activating events, "B" stands for belief systems, and "C" stands for consequences.

For example, a sales person may have found out that he or she just lost an important client and reacts with outrage, which does nothing in the effort of winning back the client. The act of being upset is the consequence, or "C." The event of losing the important customer is "A." The belief system that is causing the upset is "B."

Upon analyzing this situation, it becomes apparent that the sales person needs to work on "B," the belief system. In the instance of losing an important customer, the current belief system was to become upset and feel extreme pain over the thought of losing an important customer. If a system was in place to move toward success and calmly take the appropriate steps to either regain the business back or to find new business to supplement or replace the lost business, then stress does not have to appear.

If you had to guess in what kind of mood your doctor, or dentist, or hair stylist, or some other professional was going to be in because he or she showed up every time acting different, would you not feel uncomfortable and probably switch to another person? People look for consistency in other people's actions. You are usually able to notice when something is wrong with a person you come in contact with on a consistent basis because they are not acting the same way they usually behave. At times, they may not even notice they are acting differently. Maybe they are saying the same words they always say, but their body language, actions, and antics may be saying otherwise.

You should base your own actions and behaviors on consistency as well.

Back when I was a middle school teacher, I was asked by the principal to conduct a class on self-esteem for some children who got caught smoking. The offenders' option was to either attend my class or report for detention after school. The meetings were challenging as the offenders did not want to listen and mocked me after whatever I tried.

I initially thought that teaching this class was a bad idea, but I analyzed the situation using the ABC system and realized my belief system (B), in which I originally thought conducting the class was a bad idea, needed to be adjusted. I soon changed my belief system to concentrating on keeping up my positive efforts (planting grass) no matter how much the kids (weeds) resisted. So I tried to find something good in at least one kid each meeting and teaching that kid that there is something good in everybody.

One day Jill, a seventh grader in the group, said to me, "How can you expect me to believe in myself when I disappoint my teachers and my mother every day, so there is no way this group will help me gain self-esteem?"

I knew both myself and the student had just reached a fork in the road that could change both our lives. I repeated my phrase about planting more grass to myself and I told her, "This group finds diamonds. When you first find a diamond, it is a dull rock, but when you polish it, the rock becomes a beautiful, shining stone like no other stone on earth. We take dull rocks and bring out shining stones."

Jill made the honor roll the last nine weeks of that school year. I decided to start every group with that exact saying. We decided to have a party on the last day of the school year and when I walked into the room, I saw a huge banner the students hung there that read, "Diamonds Found And Polished Here."

The basic tenet of each example is a winning system based on consistency that was guided by an internal mental process, not an outside event. The most successful people have situations in mind that may occur in the future and how they are going to react to any crisis well in advance of having to actually face them. The reason why situations always arise is because nothing ever stays the same. So how does one stay consistent and yet address change? The answers appear throughout the rest of this manual.

"Used To Be's" Don't Make Honey

The order of the day is change. The only thing you can be sure of that will remain constant is change. Change is not part of life; change IS life. You have to accept change if you are to survive. If you readily accept change, and also take advantage of change, you will have truly developed nerves of steel

A day will never come when you will be able to sit back, relax, take a deep breath, and say to yourself, "That's it, I'm all done, and from now on, there will be no more change." Because that day will never come, do not waste any more time thinking that it will. You are kidding yourself.

The story of the International Business Machines Company is a well-known saga in the business world. IBM was considered one of the most successful businesses in the world. Big Blue was known for its consistency and its conservativeness. Remember, consistency is good, but consistency does not necessarily mean staying the same all the time, but rather being consistent dealing with change. Year after year, IBM is either the most-held stock or one of the most-held stocks in the world.

IBM changed with the times as well, but not until after receiving a huge blow to their business and their ego. They miscalculated the impact of the personal computer and remained committed to mainframes as companies like Apple beat them to market with the advent of the personal computer, and other companies such as Compaq, Dell and Gateway surpassed them in the units-sold column. IBM has recovered by addressing the modern-day needs of the consumer. Learning how to forget the past and accept change is just as important as learning new technologies.

McDonald's still makes the same hamburgers they did twenty years ago but they certainly changed with the times. As the country has become more health-conscious, McDonald's now offers salads, bottled water, and in some cities, vegetarian burgers, but they still thrive by offering their main fare of Big Macs, French fries, and Coke.

If you are not getting better every day, even if you think you are at least staying even, you are really declining. Either you are getting better every day, or you are getting worse; there is no staying on an even keel. For years, the number one employer in the country was General Motors. Today they are being challenged by temporary employment agencies such as Manpower. That should tell you that times are changing.

In 1972, the University of Pittsburgh surpassed United States Steel (U.S. Steel) as the largest employer in Pittsburgh, Pennsylvania. Few people noticed. Times were changing in Pittsburgh under everyone's noses as the city began to transform from a manufacturing economy to an economy based on educational, research, medical, technology, entertainment, and service related areas. Ten years later, most of the steel mills in Pittsburgh were blown up, dismantled, and sold for scrap as the market for domestic steel greatly diminished.

New construction is now running rampant in Pittsburgh. Two new stadiums for Pittsburgh's Major League Baseball and National Football League franchises, an addition to the city's convention center, and new headquarters for large corporations such as PNC Corporation (Bank) and Alcoa have all been recently built or are about to be finished. Thousands of tons of steel were used for these and other projects and not one ton of steel was produced in Pittsburgh (a small quantity of some specialty steel may have been produced in the Pittsburgh area). There are no more mills left to produce what is needed, so the steel is being brought in from other cities by barges and trucks.

At the turn of the last century, Pittsburgh was the steel-making capital of the world. Andrew Carnegie was the richest man in the world, thanks to income from his steel-making conglomeration, and later, from the sale of his manufacturing empire to a group headed by Charles Schwab and J.P. Morgan. By the time the next century approached, Pittsburgh was not even on the steel-making map.

Besides running from change, an alternate response is to cope with change. Coping is not enough. Quit merely coping. Embrace change, especially if it is inevitable, and you will become more exciting and innovative than you ever thought was possible.

Be First or Best by Creating a Brand

Once you accept the fact that change is inevitable, you can see change is a fun challenge. Change can represent a chance to live life with excitement and creativity. An excellent way to view change is for you to recreate yourself. Someone coined the phrase "a seven-year itch," which represents a spouse getting bored with marriage after about seven years and maybe looking outside the marriage for sexual, emotional, or relational needs.

A middle-aged business man named Paul (not his real name) came into my private practice to discuss having an affair with a woman who was one of his vendors. He asked me what my thoughts were on this idea. He said he was bored with his marriage and wanted to experience something that felt new and energized. I told him he was absolutely right, and that he needed a fresh new relationship. Paul seemed surprised at my unexpected answer but said he was glad I was agreeing with him and asked what he should do next.

I told him to go back to his wife and recreate his relationship with her (which was not the answer he wanted to hear). I told him if he had an affair he could possibly destroy at least three lives, and eventually, he would be just as bored, if not more bored, with life as he was right then.

A natural human response is to find someone attractive. Improperly acting on that response is not a good idea. If you spend the same amount of time flirting with your spouse as you would flirting with someone you want to have an affair with, chances are your spouse will pick up on your newly-found passion, and positively respond back. Then, if you get the urge to look for a new and exciting mate, recreate yourself in your relationship and you will find a new and exciting mate in your present spouse. Be more spontaneous and more creative in your present relationship and you will strengthen your relationship and raise it to heights you never thought existed.

If a relationship is abusive or destructive and cannot be changed, then by all means, end that relationship, but do not throw in the towel because you are bored. If you are bored with your relationship, chances are your spouse may feel the same way. Recreate yourself in your marriage or your relationship and you will recreate the bond you have between you and your partner.

We all get "itches" but running away from them is not the best way to scratch an itch. An itch is telling you that it is time for re-creation. Nothing will spark your nerves of steel like a little creativity. Create a new brand of you.

In one episode of the show *Seinfeld*, George Costanza realizes his life is going nowhere and decides that, if he continues to do the same things every day, his life will remain the same. So he decides on a whim to change the way he lives by doing everything opposite of what he would have normally done. He starts the day by ordering a meal at the local diner completely opposite of what he usually orders. He is instantly invigorated with confidence and creativity.

He now finds himself approaching a beautiful woman who is a complete stranger and asking her out on a date, which she accepts. He scolds guys at the movie theater who are talking too loud, actually threatening them violently. They instantly back down even though they are bigger, tougher, and outnumber him. He gets an interview with the New York Yankees through his new female acquaintance. He shows up for the job interview wearing a sweat suit. After telling off the owner of the team, George Steinbrenner, to his amazement, Steinbrenner states, "Hire this man!"

George Costanza injected some creativity into his everyday life and recreated himself. The situation is, of course, embellished for television entertainment purposes, but the theory of recreating oneself definitely deserves merit.

When was the last time you recreated yourself? A key to developing nerves of steel is to not only recreate yourself, but to keep recreating yourself. You should make every day count, because the days you have on this earth are not endless, and you never know when that last day will come.

When you think of the following names, does an image come to mind: Elvis, Madonna, Cher, Garth, Tiger? Why are they known by simply a first name? Because they are an original. They are unique in their respective professions. They all represent something we have never quite seen before. Are they the best at what they do? Maybe. Each and every one of them has figured out what people want, and they give it to the public each in their unique way; they are better than the best.

Marketing and public relations firms are paid millions of dollars annually to create brand identity for their clients. When you hear names like Elvis or Cher, or see products on a store shelf like Coke or Pepsi, you recognize the names, labels, and their associated images because these people and products, in marketing terms, are branded.

Each performer, and dozens more like them, is unique, but each has a commonality; they are creative. Elvis mixed dance and song, Madonna and Cher highlighted sexuality, Garth added a rock and roll atmosphere to country music, Tiger used his "irons" category of golf clubs where "drivers" would usually be appropriate, allowing him to control his golf shots more accurately. In each instance, attributes such as persistence, talent, education, training, etc., were all needed, but creativity was the key in setting the elite apart from the crowd.

You would have a hard time feeling burned-out or stressed-out while being truly creative at the same time. Creativity and burn-out are as incompatible as oil and water. If you are feeling stressed, burned-out, or lethargic, become creative in re-inventing yourself and you will forget any negativity even existed in your mind.

If you are burned-out at work, what can you do to serve your customers or fellow employees better? If you are bored with your relationships, how can you show your loved ones you appreciate them in a surprising way? If you are lethargic about your own life, how can you adopt a new positive, self-identity? Adopting creativity does not take loads of money or time. The more creativity you show, however, the more you will stand out as being a mover and a shaker. The late Jerry Garcia of the Grateful Dead said, *"The secret is not to be known as the best of the best, but the real secret is to be the only one who is known for what you do."*

Inject Enthusiasm and Feeling Into Your Life

Live each day with creative enthusiasm and you will feel a new and improved version of yourself emerging. How many years you have in your life is not the most important measuring tool, but rather, how much life you inject into the years you have will ultimately decide the quality of the life you live.

Your days are numbered. Because life is finite, live it as such. You are not participating in a dress rehearsal for life. Your life is your main event. The great painter Picasso painted the entire night before his death. He was enraptured about the seed that he grew inside of him. He knew that if he had limited time to live, he wanted to spend his last moments on earth doing what he loved. Picasso's passion is what made life worth living for the brilliant artist and his feelings can almost be felt by admirers of his art.

A doctor told Kathy (not her real name) she had one year to

live. She wrote the numbers 1 through 365 on her refrigerator. At the end of each day, she held a private ceremony which included asking herself what gifts she received that day before crossing off another day on her refrigerator calendar. The woman reflected daily on the enjoyment she experienced rather than focusing on the pain she was experiencing, and, in fact, she recovered and lived far beyond her one year expectancy. She decided in her mind to live and her body followed along.

Think about ten horses running wild and unharnessed in a field. What are they able to pull? Now think about the same ten horses harnessed together; what do you think they can pull? Inject enthusiasm and feeling into your life and you will feel as if you can move mountains.

How do you inject enthusiasm and feeling into your life? Act with enthusiasm and be enthusiastic about every aspect of your life, whether it be your marriage, a product you are selling, a project you are working on, a sport you are teaching to your child, or a musical instrument you are learning how to play.

Act On Your Good Ideas

Have you ever had a good idea but have never taken it any further? Have you ever thought of something you knew was a good idea but did not even write it down, only to forget about what it was later? Good ideas are constantly popping into our heads, day and night, even while we sleep.

An elderly woman was committed to a nursing home against her will. Her children felt awful but knew there was no other alternative. The elderly woman was upset for awhile, but eventually realized her fate. While sitting in the common area of the nursing home one day, she looked across the room and saw a man whom she nervously approached. She walked up to the man and said, "Excuse me, sir, but you look an awful lot like my third husband."

The man looked back at her and said, "My God, how many times have you been married before."

The woman got a twinkle in her eye, smiled and said, "Twice."

If an idea pops into your head and you feel it is a winner, act on your instincts. Your inner voice or intuition is telling you something. Do not ignore your instincts, but rather listen attentively. Some ideas may sound crazy. Just think of the ideas that popped into the heads of many great people like Martin Luther King, Nelson Mandella, Isaac Newton, Madame Curie, Thomas Edison, this list could go on for pages. What if these and other great people of history decided to just be average and not act on their instincts or listen to the great ideas that were popping into their heads?

Future parents make decisions all the time on whether to have children. The decision to have children is a drastic life-changing event, yet millions of people have children all the time. And most parents state that having children is like joining the US Marine Corps: it is the toughest job you'll ever love.

As you develop nerves of steel and begin positively affecting your life, your subconscious will start to work harder and smarter. New ideas, some of them astonishing, will begin to pop into your head. The worst thing you can do is ignore them. Realize the fact as you transform for the better, and your mind and your subconscious will be following right along. Acknowledge to yourself how astute you are now becoming and act on your good ideas. You may not be able to act out all of your ideas, but at least consider them. Keep a pencil and paper by your bedside in case a good idea pops into your head in the middle of the night and you can record it, or else you will probably forget the revelation that your mind tried to throw out at you.

Is That All The Harder You Can Hit Me?

Mohammed Ali may be one of the best athletes of all time because of the emotional and mental superiority he demonstrated during his illustrious boxing career. He was emotionally brilliant in the way he prepared for competition. When he fought George Foreman in Zaire in 1974, nobody thought Ali would win, except himself, of course. He prepared for the fight by sparring with Larry Holmes. As he covered himself up, he simply let Holmes beat up on him to toughen him up for the real fight.

Upon the opening round bell ringing on the night of the actual fight, Ali began by connecting with six of his best punches on Foreman's chin. Foreman was not phased. Ali returned to his corner at the end of the round and started talking to himself. He appeared to be discouraged, but then suddenly a revelation hit him like a light bulb turning on in his head. He changed his focus, which brought a smile on his face while sitting in his corner waiting for the next round to begin.

He came out in the next round and asked Foreman to hit him. After he did, Ali would reply not with a counter punch, but with a question, "Is that all the harder you can hit me, George?"

Ali proceeded with this strategy for the next six rounds until he sensed the discouragement in Foreman's eyes. At that moment Ali realized Foreman had become mentally and physically tired and he started to box Foreman at that point. He knew Foreman was broken. Ali won the fight.

In Earnest Hemmingway's novel *Old Man And The Sea*, the fisherman was exhausted after he went out and brought back a great fish that the sharks devoured as he was towing it in to shore.

A little boy came up to the fisherman and asked him to think about all he had lost. The fisherman agreed with the little boy but also added, "But think of all I gained."

What if you fail at a task or an endeavor? So what? Chances are good that if you failed at something, but it was new and exciting, you are probably no worse off than before you tried, and you gained the excitement and experience of breaking out of your comfort zone. Have you ever seen the bumper sticker that says, "In 100 years from now, nobody will care."

What a true statement. If you fail at something, do not focus on what you have lost; focus on what you have gained. Then conjure up your vision while keeping in mind your newly-found knowledge. Always keep your vision in front of you. Without a vision, you just may wither up and die like a piece of rotten fruit.

- **Small minds talk about people.**
- **Average minds concentrate on events.**
- **Brilliant minds formulate ideas.**

PROFILE OF STEEL

Michael worked for an investment firm in Boston. During a three-month time frame, Michael watched the stock market sink, causing investors and brokers to lose millions of dollars. Many investment firms, including Michael's firm, lost a great deal of clients as a result. But Michael focused on the positive rather than the negative. He called each and every one of his clients and asked them what he could do to help them during this tough investment climate.

They responded mostly with three areas of concern: to protect their investments, to be kept informed, and to look for investments that had become beneficial during the market downturn. Michael constantly kept his personal clients informed and asked them how he was doing on the priority list they had set up with him.

He specifically asked his clients how he was doing so they could hear themselves saying to him that he was doing a good job. After a time, when his clients had ingrained themselves with the concept that Michael was an excellent investment broker, he asked his clients to consult with their friends regarding their level of investment service. Since a great deal of those people were panicking about the downturn in the market, along with their respective brokers, Michael was able to capitalize even more by gaining additional clients through referrals.

The situation of a tough investment market did not hinder Michael from continuing to be a successful investment broker. He did not allow the event of a bad market to dictate his actions. Instead, he used his creativity, reinvented the way he did business, and excelled when others were suffering.

Do you think specific events, or rather your thoughts toward the events, are the cause of most of your feelings?

DIALOGUE OF STEEL

If Michael would have used the same attitude as most other investment brokers, his profession would have fallen on hard times along with the negative investment climate. Instead, Michael did not let the event dictate his attitude. He focused on how he could positively react to the situation.

Michael's Dialogue of Mush: I am doomed as an investment broker due to this awful market.

Michael's Dialogue of Steel: There must be an opportunity here, so how can I capitalize on the bad market instead of worrying about what the bad market may do to me?

Michael's DOM: What opportunity could possibly present itself in this market, except the opportunity to lose even more money?

Michael's DOS: I bet all my competitors are thinking about the bad market, so I am going to focus on my clients instead of the market and I will be well ahead of most of my competition right from the start.

Michael's DOM: How can I help my clients who are upset since for most of them it is raining losses, not profits?

Michael's DOS: Exactly, allow me to provide the umbrella and rain hat!

Michael's DOM: How can I possibly provide protection for my clients? What would they want from me?

Michael's DOS: I won't know until I ask them, so I will do just that, by asking every one of them.

Events do not cause our feelings. Rather, our thoughts toward events dictate how we feel.

NUTS AND BOLTS FROM NERVES OF STEEL - FLOOR THREE
How To Plant Grass Rather Than Pull Weeds

No matter what you are trying to accomplish, you need a system to accomplish your endeavor. Ask yourself what the best process is to achieve your desired outcome. Your answer will be the keys to a winning system. Your system should include consistency, because without consistency, you will not stay motivated enough to successfully continue your journey.

If you make small improvements to yourself every day, you will amaze yourself about how far you have come in a certain time period. Seize each day and notice the positive changes that are taking place. They will serve as a motivator for you in the future. If you feel yourself becoming stagnant, recreate yourself. There is no right or wrong way of recreating yourself. Only you know the best way to recreate yourself. Recreate yourself in different ways. Inject some creativity in your life. Have some fun.

Remember that positive and negative occurrences will constantly happen in your life. You will have no control over many of these events, so why worry about them or let them affect your life? The event will not dictate your life. How you react to the event will dictate your success or failure in the future just as your reactions have affected you in the past.

FLOOR FOUR
How To Get Tougher On Life Instead of Wishing Life Was Easier On You

"It is better to trust all the time and sometimes be disappointed than to trust none of the time and always be miserable." **Abraham Lincoln**

What Happens Is Not Everything

There was a woman who tragically lost her three-year-old son in a San Diego, California, McDonald's restaurant when a man walked in and sprayed the restaurant with machine gun bullets. She discussed in a magazine interview her focus on life after that awful event. She stated that she had put the past behind her because it could not be brought back. She also stated that she did not focus on the future because there was no way of knowing how much future is left. She simply focused on each day as it arrived, lived each day to its fullest, and considered each day on earth a gift, or a present. "That is why it is called the 'present,'" she said.

How You Treat What Happens Is Everything

This story should alleviate the need for you to be bothered by trivialities in life. If someone can get over the senseless, cold-blooded murder of their three-year-old child, you can get over small problems or dilemmas that creep up in your life.

I had to speak at a hospital one morning on the topic of the importance of forgiving others. After my talk, a woman walked up to me still furious at the people who had just laid her friend

off and was almost as furious at me for suggesting the idea of forgiving others at a time when she was still steaming over the loss of her friend's job.

I then gave the same talk at the hospital that afternoon. This time another woman walked up to me afterwards. She began to cry as she told me what happened to her and her family on Easter Sunday. She and her husband along with their young son and daughter planned a flight in the small private airplane they had just bought, but the plane never made it off the ground during takeoff. She and her daughter escaped, but her husband and son were not so lucky. She was glad that she lived so she could be instrumental in the raising of her daughter and was also thankful to all the people who helped her, including me, who thought my talk meant a great deal to her.

How can two people feel so differently? One thinks life is awful while another accepts what life has dealt them and moves on. The answer is simple. Events do not make one feel. How one chooses to accept each event is the key. If you trust in yourself and our ability to cope, then you know you can make it through whatever life throws at you. If you feel a current dilemma is too much for you to cope with on your own, seek out the appropriate help.

Nerves of steel and trust go hand-in-hand. If you find a mentor who shows you a good process for reaching goals, you must trust. You may find at times that you want to adjust your process, but once you feel you have perfected a system, you have to trust it.

Trust

Quarterback Pete Gonzalez arrived in the NFL in 1998 via free agency from the University of Pittsburgh to the Pittsburgh Steelers.

While at Pitt, he was not named the starting quarterback until his senior season but emerged as one of the top quarterbacks in the conference. Once he began to trust, he immediately rose from bench-warmer and quarterback of the scout team to throwing for over 2800 yards his senior season, including 30 touchdowns, 7 in one game, which surpassed a record held by future NFL Hall-of-Famer Dan Marino, a former University of Pittsburgh alumnus.

The culmination of Gonzalez' college career came to a head during his last regular-season contest as a collegian, which was at rival West Virginia University. A Pitt victory was mandatory to keep its bowl game hopes alive. The game was neck-and-neck as all four quarters ended, leading to not one overtime, or even two, but three overtime periods.

The Mountaineers took a 38-35 lead in the third overtime, giving the Panthers one last crack to win. And that crack was squeezed slimmer and slimmer as Pitt was faced with fourth down and nineteen yards to go for the first down. Pete walked up to the line to take the snap as 40,000 opposing fans screamed at the top of their lungs. Just before the play began, a shade of doubt entered Pete's head, but he ignored it, trusted in his coaching and his instinct to make the right play as he thought to himself, "You know what you have to do, now get it done."

He completed the most important pass in his collegiate career, which he was then able to follow about thirty seconds later with the touchdown pass that won the game for him and the Panthers.

"On paper he was not supposed to be able to complete a fourth and nineteen," said West Virginia Head Coach Don Nehlen after the game. "Can you believe that? He completed a fourth and nineteen!"

Before the start of the 1997 college football season, new University of Pittsburgh head football coach Walt Harris asked me to talk to a quarterback, Pete Gonzalez. The first time I met with Pete, he started to cry. I asked him why he was crying. He said he just buried his father. He then went on to say his life did not work because, in his opinion, he did not trust. He did not listen if a teacher or coach tried to tell him something. Pete also did not trust himself. Other people had hurt him in the past, giving him reason not to trust, but he said to me that he knew, if he wanted his life to work, he had to trust.

He began, with great effort, to trust other people, himself, and a higher calling. He began to absorb what the new coach was trying to teach him, a coach that specialized in teaching quarterbacks and had been a mentor to former NFL quarterbacks such as Tony Eason and Boomer Esiason.

Nellie King, after retiring from his job as the Pittsburgh Pirate baseball radio announcer, was hired at Duquesne University in Pittsburgh to coach the golf team. He tells his students to "see it, feel it, trust it." In other words, they have to see the line of the shot before they hit the ball, then feel it in their forearms and wrists, and then trust that the ball will take the best path after they hit it. This formula spells success. Does the ball always go in? No. But it goes in a lot more often than when hit by people who do not trust.

When Nellie explained to me his system of trust, I asked him if there was any better system to use while golfing. He commented for me to think about Lee Trevino's swing, which is technically awful, but works for Lee. He told me that the secret is not to find the perfect swing, but to find a swing that works perfect for you, and then to trust that the swing will not let you down.

Trust can be hard at times, but it can be developed. Research the best process to do whatever you want to accomplish, and then trust your findings. Trust the people who are teaching you something. Trust the internal calling of your seed.

The first day I worked for the Dallas Cowboys, then-head coach Chan Gailey asked me what I thought was the major factor in a team being a success, and I responded, "Trust, because if the players trust in what the coach is trying to do, trust in each other, and in themselves, they will win."

Levels of Trust

If you cannot trust yourself, who can you trust? Every time you say "I can't," you are casting doubts regarding your own abilities. You are demonstrating the lowest level of trust in yourself. Even if you say to yourself, "I will try," you are still casting doubts about your potential for success.

During the *Star Wars* movie *The Empire Strikes Back*, there is a scene where Yoda commands Luke Skywalker to lift his wrecked space fighter out of the swamp merely using telepathy. Luke says that he will try and Master Yoda snaps back that it is not good enough to merely try, that one must actually do. Yoda put it less eloquently when he stated, "No try, do!"

The next level of trust is saying to yourself, "I will." You are perceiving that you will put forth the effort and will try your approach for some time, but when it gets rocky, you have a good chance of abandoning your efforts. In order to be successful, you must trust yourself at the highest level.

You will be placing the ultimate level of trust in yourself when you say to yourself, "I commit, and I will stick with this system and make it work." This ultimate level of self-trust is where nerves of steel are molded. This upper echelon of commitment is what Yoda was referring to when he instructed Luke Skywalker not to simply try, but to do. Don't just *decide* to do something. Do it instead. Deciding and actually accomplishing a task or a goal are two different actions.

I once had a client with cancer who was given a fifty-fifty chance of recovery. I asked her what she was going to do to enhance her chances. She outlined a change in her lifestyle, including a better diet and strong use of prayer. I then asked her what she would do if her system did not work and she answered, "Then I will die with faith."

Do Not Feel Sorry For Yourself

Feeling sorry for yourself is one of life's greatest temptations. Many of your past difficulties are results of life biting into your expectations. Sometimes you expect the world to conduct itself in a certain manner. When just the opposite actually occurs, the door to stress and worry is thrown wide open. You can either slam the door in front of you, or you can have pity on yourself while you are sucked through the door.

Establish in your mind that life is not easy and getting what you want may be even harder, or sometimes just not in the cards at all. If you determine that what you want is worth the effort, and you commit yourself to exert the necessary effort, you are on your way down the pathway of success. Walking the path of success is not always easy, but the fulfillment of a great relationship, the rearing of wonderful children, the development of a rewarding career, or the realization of an endeavor personal to you is worth the effort.

Every goal has a price. If you accept that fact, you are on your way to reaching whatever goal or goals you put in front of yourself.

When Nelson Mandella was imprisoned, he never felt sorry for himself because he realized the price he was paying was necessary in his fight to end apartheid in South Africa.

Once you accept the fact that the world does not get better, rather you must get better in reacting to the world, the more prepared you will be to face the world. Expect things to be difficult at times. Once you raise the level of your expectations, being immediately satisfied in life is probably not going to be a reality. As you work on making your dreams come true, you may suffer some hard times. Get used to being uncomfortable at times and you will be able to stretch well beyond your current comfort zone.

Extending beyond one's prior limits is usually painful for most people. Participants have answered in many surveys that they would rather die than speak in front of an audience. Why? Speaking in front of an audience is a huge stretch beyond most people's comfort zone.

Positive self-esteem is a concept many in the pop psychology field believe leads to the development of positive people. Most everyone is born with some positive attributes such as creativity or athletic ability that can raise self-esteem. Without the discipline to think positively during tough times, however, positive self-esteem can easily be eaten away by stress, worry, depression, or worse. Many of us suffer today from "Burger King" syndrome, we always want it "our way." If things do not go our way, we feel sorry for ourselves.

When you begin to feel sorry for yourself, listen to the voice of strength inside of you to guide you past the uncomfortable times. Muster enough strength to see yourself through the tough times when they occur, because tough times will be constantly occurring for the rest of your life, but you have the ability to choose not to shrivel up when tough times do occur.

There Is No Such Thing As The Good Old Days

If you let yourself believe that things are tough today and are only getting tougher, you will never have a grasp on your perception of the world. Do not fall into the trap that the world was a better place years ago. Children know more now in the sixth grade than some adults knew twenty or thirty years ago.

Present-day school children are faced with devastating violence, guns, drugs, sex, and a plethora of other dilemmas. Half of all marriages in America end in divorce. The workplace is becoming more challenging as people are laid off in droves while the remaining employees are expected to continue adding more duties to their work day. Downsizing, merging, streamlining, restructuring, these are words that were not in corporate vocabulary only decades ago. Many people work harder to earn less. If only things were like they were in the "good old days."

Sound familiar? Let's take a real hard look at the so-called "good old days." During the seventies, double-digit inflation spun out of control. During the sixties (and half of the seventies), the Vietnam War hung over the country like a dark cloud. During the fifties, the population was constantly worried about being blown off the face of the earth by Russian atomic weapons. People during the forties saw World War II affect most of the world and devastate or obliterate parts of it.

During the thirties, the country struggled through a depression like an elephant caught in a quagmire. During the twenties, the country was engulfed in prohibition which sparked the development of organized crime. During the teens, the world witnessed the senseless slaughter year-after-year of thousands of young troops on the battlefields of Europe during World War I. Before the turn of the century, America's Civil War caused more American casualties than any other war the United States fought.

So when did these so-called "good-old-days" supposedly occur? You get the picture. There are no such things as "good old days," only your perception that things in the past were always better. The world you live in, no matter what time-frame, is a fact of life. Once you accept the reality that your surroundings are not responsible for your happiness, the easier you can understand that the key to life is not what happens around you, but how you react to what happens around you.

Perception Can Be Greater Than The Truth

What is perceived to be true can often project a stronger image than the actual truth. Police officers investigating a crime scene will oftentimes question witnesses and receive conflicting stories. Is this dilemma caused by witnesses purposely lying? Usually not, but different people perceive events differently. You see the world through your own rose-colored glasses.

According to Gregory (1977), a middle-aged cataract patient had been blind since birth, but at the age of fifty-two, a successful operation granted the man his sight. For his entire life, the previously-blind man's perception of the world was how he received his surroundings from what he heard or felt. He once attempted to jump out of a fourth-story window in order to get a closer look at traffic, not realizing the consequences of his actions. He did not know how to react to his recent gift.

He soon became depressed by the difficulties he was now presented with due to his sight being corrected. He found the absence of light to be more soothing and would spend countless hours siting in complete darkness. He was now bombarded with so much unfamiliar information that he could not handle the massive change, or his perception of the world around him.

Turnbull (1961) tells of a story in the *American Journal of Psychology* where he transplants a pygmy from the rain forest to the African plains. The pygmy always saw his world through the dense foliage of a rain forest and had never seen objects from a great distance.

He did not know what to make of a herd of buffalo seen thundering across a plain from miles away, and thus thought he saw a swarm of insects. He was even more confused as he was driven closer to the buffalo and his so-called "insects" magically transformed into buffalo.

How many times have you witnessed sporting events where fans of the losing team blame officials? How often do fans of the team that wins a sporting event complain about the officiating?

Hastorf and Cantril (1954) conducted a study where Dartmouth and Princeton students watched a college football game film in which a Princeton student was injured. The Dartmouth students felt the game was equally played, and both teams were equally penalized. The Princeton students described the game as "rough and dirty," blaming the opponent who injured the Princeton player as committing twice the number of penalties.

Believe in Yourself but Cut the Cards

When you believe you are the master of your own destiny, according to Bandura (1986), and are able to meet demanding challenges head on, you are self-efficacious. People who have self-efficacy bounce back from failures and approach challenges asking how to handle what has happened instead of worrying what else could go wrong.

People with nerves of steel believe in themselves. Problems will arise. By tapping into your inner strength, you can face your problems with confidence without being arrogant. There is a difference between confidence and arrogance. Professional athletes can fall into the trap of confusing confidence with arrogance.

Professional athletes prepare hard for each performance and sometimes play well as a result. But the athletes that start to lose focus on the task at hand and fall into the trap of bragging about being all-pro, or worrying if their next contract will be enough, or how much their next signing bonus will be are not being confident, but being arrogant. Arrogance can mean disaster for a professional athlete.

How many athletes in any sport began their professional careers fantastic, (or in some cases, never got their careers underway) but fizzled out almost as quickly? When you add all the musical artists that have recorded songs over the last fifty years, how many musical artists wrote and recorded hit song after hit song, compared to artists who are referred to as "one-hit wonders"?

Most emotions have their place. Fear should appear in one's life probably as much as confidence, or you would be jumping off of bridges or driving through guard rails. Problems arise when you have too much of an emotion which can run or ruin your life. The secret to using your emotions to your greatest advantage is displaying the right emotion in the right amount at the right time. Get tough by talking to yourself. Focus through the frustration of the growing pains of mastering your emotions.

Psychologist Albert Ellis (1988) defined a condition in which people think they cannot tolerate pain, discomfort or adversity as low frustration tolerance. When you suffer from low frustration tolerance, you often lose focus on what you are trying to accomplish and eventually abandon your goal. It is not the discomfort, therefore, that slows your progress, but what you are telling yourself about the discomfort. If you are preventing yourself from getting everything out of life you possibly can, or if you are bored with life, or suffer from serious depression or high anxiety, you may have low frustration tolerance.

When a dilemma arises in which you tell yourself you can't stand it, or you just can't take it anymore, try telling yourself you can stand it by toughening up.

Patch Your Roof While It Is Still Warm Outside

A man went to see his very ill friend who was probably living one of his last days. The man bent over his friend, held his hand and asked him how he was doing. The sick man answered back in a very low voice, "I am doing fine because I patched my roof when it was warm outside."

He prepared for his death by readying his spirit earlier in his life while he was still in good health.

PROFILE OF STEEL

Young Ken Dorsey was the starting quarterback for the University of Miami Hurricane football team during the 2000 season. Cleveland Brown head coach Butch Davis was Miami's head coach at the time. Prior to the 2000 season, Davis had never beaten the Florida State Seminoles during his tenure at Miami.

The Hurricanes faced a Seminole team ranked number one in the country that year and starred Heisman Trophy winner Chris Wenke at quarterback. The temperature at game time was 97 degrees. The Hurricanes led for most of the four hour and twenty minute contest, preserving their lead with several defensive stops inside their own five yard line. With less than two minutes remaining in the game, however, Wenke drove the Seminoles down the field to score a touchdown and take the lead.

After the Hurricanes received the ensuing kickoff, Dorsey approached the huddle thinking that, if he trusted himself and his coaches, and focused on one play at a time, he would be able to lead his team to one last score and pull a victory from the jaws of defeat before the clock ended that day. That is precisely what happened.

Do you have enough trust in yourself to rise to any occasion?

DIALOGUE OF STEEL

Ken Dorsey could have thrown in the towel and given up, but he came too far in that game, and in life to let the victory slip away. Dorsey used his inner dialogue to fight off the negativity that would have allowed him to lose trust in himself and his abilities, talking himself out of a victory.

*Ken's **Dialogue of Mush**: I can't believe they scored and took the lead this late in the game after all we went through to try to win.*

*Ken's **Dialogue of Steel**: Don't judge the past, even if the past just happened two minutes ago. Focus on the current task at hand.*

*Ken's **DOM**: But how can we win now with so little time left against such a good team?*

*Ken's **DOS**: The game has not ended yet. Don't prejudge the outcome. Stay on course.*

*Ken's **DOM**: But I am so tired, and my teammates are so tired after this hard fought battle that we have nothing left to give.*

*Ken's **DOS**: My body has more in it than I realize. If I feel absolutely positive about this, it should rub off on my teammates as well.*

*Ken's **DOM**: What if the clock runs out before I get the job done?*

*Ken's **DOS**: Take one play at a time. And trust.*

Do not argue with a tired and discouraged mind; you will lose every time. The more you focus on the task at hand, the less room will be available in your mind for negative thoughts to emerge and disrupt your efforts.

NUTS AND BOLTS FROM NERVES OF STEEL - FLOOR FOUR
How To Get Tougher On Life Instead of Wishing Life Was Easier On You

You have probably experienced some tough times in the past, experiences that you felt were devastating at the time. Now that you look back, you realize you were strong enough to face catastrophes and come out okay. You have to trust your instincts as you face tough decisions or circumstances in the present and future. Listen to your inner voice. Chances are you will be led in the right direction.

Most importantly, are you prepared mentally and spiritually if an emergency would occur? No matter what situation may arise, trust in your abilities and your intuition to guide you through the good times as well as the bad times. Stop wasting time pitying yourself if you think times are tough. Instead, decide to do something about the tough times if you are currently facing any.

When you make a decision to take certain actions, to either combat tough times, or to improve your life, do not simply think about taking those actions, actually commit to taking them, or you will meander your way through life.

FLOOR FIVE
How To Stop, Walk, and Then Run In Order To Avoid Coasting

"So my advice is simple, figure out what your priorities are and say no to everything else." - **Elaine St. James**

A Broken Focus Is the Main Reason for Failure

During the 1998 American League Championship series, New York Yankee pitcher David Wells was warming up before the game. Opponents' fans began shouting obscenities at him about his mother. The fans were adults and their children, after witnessing this demonstration of disrespect, followed suit. Ordinarily, this behavior would not have bothered him, but his mother recently passed away.

He started the game, but was focusing more on how much he would like to confront the hecklers instead of the opposing batters. His initial performance was disastrous. After giving up a number of hits in the first inning, he walked back to the dugout and had a talk with himself. He addressed his lack of focus and decided to get back on track with the task at hand, which was to get out opposing batters.

After sharpening his focus, he pitched the rest of the game almost perfectly, leading the Yankees to victory. He actually thanked the hecklers in public after the game for motivating him to stay focused and perform to the best of his abilities.

The best way to overcome adversity is to perform, enjoy, and get completely wrapped up in your goals and current tasks. Former First Lady Ladybird Johnson once said, "The way to overcome shyness is to become so wrapped up in something that you forget to be afraid."

An American doctor who arrived first on the scene of a jetliner crash was caring for seriously injured passengers to the best of his ability. Most of the injured were Columbian and the doctor did not speak Spanish. As he witnessed people with limbs hanging from their torso, all he could understand was their cries for a doctor.

After the tragedy, the doctor was asked how he could concentrate with all the noise of sirens, helicopters, and chaos going on around him. He answered back, "What noise? That was the most quiet environment I ever worked in."

One afternoon, I was talking to Peter Skudra, a one-time goalie for the Pittsburgh Penguins of the National Hockey League. The Penguins were preparing to face the New York Rangers, who were led at the time by hockey legend Wayne Gretzky.

"It will be hard stopping Gretzky, he's the greatest player of them all," commented Skudra. I thought for a moment, then told him, "Peter, you do not have to stop Gretzky, you have to stop the puck, so just stay focused and keep telling yourself to see the puck and then stop the puck and you'll do fine. Gretzky is not your problem."

When you focus to the point that you are completely wrapped up in what you are doing, peak experiences will take place almost magically. Remember the story of Thomas Edison. He would focus on his experiments to the degree that he would lose track of his days and nights. He worked hours upon hours because he loved what he was doing, not because he was forced to perform his experiments by an employer or himself.

Rick Seebak, a public television station producer in Pittsburgh, has been creating documentaries for over twenty years. His earlier documentaries featured famous places and landmarks in and around Pittsburgh, such as bridges, amusement parks, and skyscrapers. He has since expanded on a national level and has addressed hot dog stands, old amusement parks, and flea markets. He commented, that when he was putting the finishing touches on his productions, he would be so focused that he would forget to look at the clock and could not believe 16 hours had passed.

"I just love the work that I am doing so much that I lose all track of time because I am so focused and buried in my project," Seebak said. "I can't imagine, nor do I have any desire to move up in management, switch professions, or do anything else that would distract me or take me away from doing the work I love."

If a work day drags on, you may be in the wrong line of work. If you look up at the clock and realize the day flew by and you enjoyed the work you did, that is a good sign you may be in the right line of work for you.

A nurse stopped by my private office because she was having problems giving the wrong medication to patients. I asked her if anything was going on in her life that might be a distraction and she commented that she was facing some challenging times with her teenage daughter. She was being distracted at work so I helped her to refocus on the task at front of her while she was on duty, which was serving her patients.

It is easy just to say to stay focused and go for it, and you will get to where you want to go, but staying focused when you have nothing to keep focused on is merely a hollow concept. If you are not participating in activities or a profession you have no interest in, you are not physically capable of staying focused to the point that you are passionate about what you are doing. So stop for a few minutes and take a good hard look at what you are doing, at your place of employment, in your relationship, at your church, if you participate in organized religion, with your children. Are you accomplishing what you want to by living life to its fullest? Are you answering your calling in life?

Your Time Is Your Wealth

Most people have the wrong idea about what real wealth means. Your true wealth is not your monetary wealth, but your time. Nobody knows how long they have to walk on this earth. You only have a certain amount of time, so you should spend what little time you have as wisely as you can.

I once conducted a seminar for wealthy executives. I explained to them a scenario that had them picture they were on their death beds with one week to live, but I had a miracle drug that would cure them, but the cost was their entire fortune. I asked if anyone would be willing to pay the price for the miracle drug. Every hand in the room went up.

Think of your life like a bank account. Tomorrow you will have one less day in your account and there is absolutely nothing you can do to bring back the day you lost. You can only begin to live today and the days in the future like they are your last days on earth. Remember, betting you will live forever is a losing bet every time. Why not live a life you can look back on someday and say you loved living?

Fall In Love

Maurice Sendak wrote the children's book *Where The Wild*

Things Are. He drew a rendition of one of his "wild thing" beasts on a card and sent it to a child. The child loved the drawing so much he ate it. He did not care about the monetary value of an original Sendak drawing. He loved it, so he ate it. Passion is a hunger within us which calls us to behave like this child, to figure out what it is we love to do and feel so much passion for it that we eat it up.

Mary Ellen Mark is a world-acclaimed photographer who has had pictures published in many magazines including *Life, Rolling Stone,* and the *New Yorker*. She has earned numerous awards for her breath-taking photography. When asked what makes her a great photographer, she answered back that the passion she has for her work is why she dedicates herself to her art.

"You have to be obsessed, consumed by wanting to do a great job," Mark said. "After all these years of taking pictures, being a photographer is still what I care for most."

When was the last time you really sat down with yourself and asked yourself if you are doing what you love? Have you ever asked yourself that? Your life is too short and too valuable to waste it and let it go by while you toil in endeavors you hate just because you feel you have to make a living, or have to behave a certain way in a relationship, or have to act a certain way. Everybody needs their "68" in life, just as National Hockey League player Jaromir Jagr uses as his motivating force in spending his life doing what he loves, playing hockey.

Most people spend more hours planning their wedding than they spend planning their life together. Have you ever sat down with your spouse and discussed goals for your life together? Have you developed a plan and put deadlines on steps in your plan? If you have not, why not? A common answer, and one that usually comes to mind is, "I don't have time," or "I just never found the time."

You do not have enough time not to find what you are passionate about in life and implement a plan to live out your dreams. Everybody was put on this earth to achieve something. Find out what your assigned achievement is and start achieving. Put worries aside, such as I need to make a living or I need to support my family with whatever job I can find. If you find your passion in life, making a living will find you.

When Dick Ponzi talks about wine, one realizes he is talking about his passion for life. His Oregon wines have won prizes many times over. When asked how he became a wine grower, he answered, "I was an aerospace engineer, but ever since my childhood, I never let go of my love of wines and how to make them, which was what my family did."

He let go of his engineering job, followed his passion for wine making, loaded all his belongings on a flatbed truck, and drove to Oregon in search of starting his wine business. He continued, "Wines are magical. The most exciting thing about wines is that they can bring rewarding surprises sometimes because they are so unpredictable, and when they come out great, they just over excite me."

Ponzi never mentions all the bad wines he created in search of a winning combination. He focuses on the good aspect of the unpredictability of a batch of wine. Instead of mentioning that sometimes the wine turns out bad, he looks forward to the excitement that overcomes him when a batch turns out good. He has his picture in his mind of being a good wine producer and he is eating up his vision of life. Ponzi committed himself to follow his calling in life.

Louis V. Gerstner, the CEO of the IBM Corporation, referred to such strong commitments that are possible in human nature when he said, "No machine can replace the human spark which is made up of spirit, compassion, love, and understanding."

Do not worry if you are in no position right now to quit a job you hate, or take a vacation with your family, or become more active with your children or at your church. Just start to recreate yourself and focus on developing a plan which allows you to live life according to how you WANT to live life, rather than how you think you MUST live life. You have to start walking before you can run. Good things will start to happen.

The Broken Focus Pattern

Most human beings act the same when the report comes from the brain that screams, "I am in danger!"

The message has the same results on your body regardless of whether you are worried about winning a game, trying to beat a deadline, racing to get to work without being late, running from a potential mugger, smelling smoke and thinking your house is on fire, having just asked a stranger to dance, or trying to avoid being involved in an accident.

The "danger" message begins as an impulse taken in by one or a combination of your senses and then triggers an impulse in your brain. The brain then excites various regions on our body such as our skin, heart, and lungs to produce an alarming sensation. Symptoms may occur such as a palpitating heart, sweaty palms, or heavy breathing. You may also feel a tingling in your stomach, more commonly called butterflies in the stomach.

Your nerves are causing these sensations via a chemical called adrenaline, which is released at the nerve terminals in the affected organs. A rush of adrenaline is also released into the bloodstream to enhance actions of the sympathetic nervous system. Such a rush of adrenaline may even lead to superhuman actions. We have all heard stories such as mothers lifting cars or telephone poles off their injured children during a crisis situation.

Such chemical imbalances may have been useful to the human race at one time. Ancient humans may have needed the rush of adrenaline to kill their next meal during a hunt, or try to prevent someone or something else from making a meal out of them, or outrun a predator. Such dangers are no longer prevalent in our everyday lives, but the biological mechanisms still linger.

Barkow, Cosmides, and Tooby (1992) felt that many specialized parts have developed within our brain, each evolving as a reasoning-coping mechanism during millions of years as hunters and gatherers. The fear reactions, however, are still part of our nature and are usually found to be more of a hindrance than helpful.

The Apollo 13 voyage to space was doomed before it completed its mission. An onboard explosion caused malfunctions that seriously damaged the chances of the astronauts safe return to earth. Although his life and those of his fellow astronauts were suddenly in jeopardy, mission Captain Jim Lovell calmly reported to mission control on earth, "Houston, I think there's a problem here."

Lovell was evidently taking immediate charge of the situation. He must have felt a rush of adrenaline when he realized the space capsule was in sudden danger. He ignored the distraction, however, and proceeded to act accordingly and not lose his nerves. The tone of his voice and the level of his performance was proof that he controlled his body by controlling his thinking and by focusing.

A woman I once worked with named Debbie (not her real name) wanted to move up the company ladder in the field of mortgage banking. She had to make enough proper contacts and sell her product to enough banks that she would meet or exceed her quota. If she accomplished such a feat, she would be promoted and would also receive an award at the company's annual meeting. She began to focus on not messing up instead of focusing on her main task of contacting decision-makers at banks who would lead to potential sales. Ultimately, things DID go wrong.

So she decided to change her way of thinking. She placed a picture of a woman in a red dress on her refrigerator and imagined that she would wear the same dress at the annual meeting ceremony where she would receive her award. She developed a plan of reaching a certain number of contacts each day and focused on selling products instead of making her quota. As a result of working her new plan, the results fell into place, which were above quota. Debbie received her promotion and was presented with an award at the company's annual meeting, in which she accepted while wearing a red dress.

If you let distractions get to you, more harm than good will ultimately occur. After tackling him for the first time in a professional football game, former Pittsburgh Steeler linebacker Levon Kirkland would often whisper in the opposing running back's ear that every time he touches the ball he is going to get hit and tackled. If the opponent had let Kirkland's threats get to him, by the time the second half approached, he may have been playing at a substandard level because he would have allowed too much adrenaline to flow in at attempt to make him fight harder. This distraction would divert the opponent's focus from the game.

Research has shown that athletes playing in a focused, positive frame of mind will outperform athletes playing recklessly and without focus. If you stay calm, positive, and focused on the task at hand, you can control a good portion of your nervous system and avoid the release of too much distracting adrenaline.

Once you develop the power to focus, your walk through life will begin to turn into a trot. If you stay focused, your trot will transform into a gallop through life and you will be amazed at how much your life has changed for the better compared to when you began your new-found journey.

If God Drew This House, How Would He Draw It?

Frank Lloyd Wright, the renowned architect, is known for many extraordinary creations, including "Falling Water," located near Uniontown, Pennsylvania. This magnificent residential complex served as the summer home of Pittsburgh's Kaufmann Family, founders of Kaufmann's Department Store. The family wanted the house to be built in the proximity of the natural waterfall, which was created by a stream running through the property.

They thought Wright would build the house adjacent to the waterfall so house guests could look out the window and see the falls. Instead, Wright designed the house to be built **over** the falls, an unbelievable feat of architecture. The design was achieved by using cantilever technology, each layer of the main structure set like drawers on top of each other.

Wright left no stone unturned as far as the design of the house and its furnishings. He coordinated every detail, even down to the desk chairs and table lamps.

Wright taught architecture at his studio/home in Phoenix. He would tell his students right before they put pen to paper, "If God were drawing this house, how would he draw it?"

One of the highest purposes of our work is finding the work we were chosen to perform. Your work can then become a metaphor of something higher than a paycheck if you are performing what you feel is your calling in life. The next time you begin your day at work, ask yourself, "If God were raising or teaching this child, selling this product, or building this building, how would he do it?"

Dr. Martin Luther King said, "If a man is called to be a street sweeper, he should sweep the streets with the same passion as Michaelangelo when he painted, or Beethoven when he conducted music, or Shakespeare when he wrote plays. He should sweep streets so well that all the hosts of Heaven and earth will pause to say, Here is a great street sweeper who did his job well."

Jimmy Carter, President of the United States at the time, was working with a Cuban pastor who has had unbelievable results with poor Puerto Rican immigrants. President Carter asked this pastor how he was achieving such extraordinary results when so many others were not able to be successful. The pastor looked at President Carter and said, "Senoir Jimmy, it is important that we always love two people, God and whoever is in front of us at the time." The man had found the work he was called to do and performed his work at a level he thought God would perform.

A nurse worked to her highest level of excellence while assisting a mother in having her first baby. The mother tried to have a baby for the longest time, but until now, was never able to have children. When the baby was born, the nurse noticed the baby had no arms. It was this nurse who was given the task of presenting the baby to the parents after the doctor broke the horrifying news. She concentrated on doing her job as if God was doing it. She calmly walked into the room, and gently handed the baby to the mother. The mother held up the baby, and said, "We are so glad you are here. God must have known we need you infinitely more than you will ever need us. Please teach us whatever we need to learn. We welcome you into our lives."

As the nurse walked out of the room, she was sure, without any doubt, that God was in that room with them. No paycheck was worth what she experienced that day.

Focus on the Solution Rather Than Concentrating on the I'm's

Dweck and Licht (1980) demonstrated that among children who perceived the cause of classroom difficulties as permanent (such as I'm dumb and that is that) learned less than children who perceived the cause of classroom difficulties as temporary (I didn't try hard enough this time but I'm able to try harder the next time). Helpless children judge themselves as failures while children who had hope focused on remedies rather than the actual failures.

Similarly, leaders who believe that the success of their organization depends on their ability to lead are much more successful than leaders who think their success depends mainly on the ability of those they are leading. The art of parenting can fall under the same perception. Parents can become more beneficial to their children if the parents believe it is their positive parenting that will lead to positive children, rather than the ability of the child to be positive. Good children are not a result of genetics, a neighborhood, or a school system. Good children are a result of good parents.

If you believe you can make a difference in this world, you can make your own reality. If you truly believe you can influence events you attend, the work you participate in and the people around you, oftentimes you can. If you come up with an excuse why you cannot sell, why you cannot parent, why you cannot be better in your relationships, you are writing your own destiny on the wall.

Unsuccessful salespeople often come up with excuses for their sales managers as to why they are not reaching their quota, such as they are working in the wrong territory, their compensation plan needs to be fixed, their products need updated. These sales people usually remain unsuccessful even after changes are made to alter what was perceived as being hindrances.

A man came to see me after his marriage had failed. He told me he was an alcoholic. He then told me he was depressed. Finally, he told me he was a real loser. I thought to myself how hard he worked at diagnosing himself. He believed his plight because he put "I'm" in front of his dilemmas, such as "I'm an alcoholic," or "I'm depressed," or "I'm a real loser."

Focus on solutions to your problems rather than labeling yourself with negative "I'm's," such as "I'm too stupid," or "I'm too poor," or "I'm not attractive." If you use too many "I'm's" you may lock yourself into a diagnosis that is not even true of yourself. If you believe it to be true, however, it is as good as being true. Some mental health professionals question the value of a diagnosis, because a label is place, on someone following a diagnosis, which may hinder the problem-solving process.

Repeated studies of successful people in either business or sports reveal they have cue words for themselves. Those cue words help them stay focused on what is important to them. They do not waste time playing games with themselves such as the "I'm" game or the "what-if" game (what if I fail, or what will people think of me if I do this) according to Fair and Lynette (1992).

If you model yourself after successful people by practicing the same positive habits they practice, you have a much better chance of experiencing a positive life as well.

People who live life using nerves of steel do not judge outcomes or consequences. They are focused on developing a process to achieve their goals and then taking the actions stated in their plans. Successful people use their cue words to keep their goals and actions firmly embedded in their minds, goals and actions based on their internal seeds. Examples of cue words may be "focus on the task" or "stay on target."

You have a better chance of winning at the game of life by developing the language of winning. Consider what you need to be successful, but only consider what will also make you happy. Examples may be serving others, improving yourself, growing stronger, listening to others, becoming more spiritual. Let the hunger inside of you become exposed to you and others.

Frequently ask yourself during each day the following question, "Is what I am doing right now getting me to where I need to be?" Focus on what you truly want and the answer to your daily question will ring loudly in your head.

By developing your inner voice, you will be able to stay focused on your course to success, to develop nerves of steel. Talk to yourself. Be your own best coach on life. Keep telling yourself to stay focused on what is important and try to use as much energy on those activities.

Don't Coast Through Life

I was in tenth grade algebra class on the second day of school. When the teacher turned around to write on the board, a kid name Charlie stood up next to his desk and pretended to start up a motorcycle. He then proceeded to ride his pretend motorcycle around the room three times, even pulling a wheelie in front of the teacher. After he stopped and parked his pretend motorcycle, the teacher sent him to the principal's office. He walked out of the room, returned to pick up his motorcycle, and promptly went down to the principal's office. After this episode, I befriended Charlie and we became best friends.

About twenty years later, Charlie was attacked with a virus that affected his nervous system leaving the doctors to wonder if he would ever walk again. While in the rehabilitation hospital, Charlie began by strengthening his arms and especially his wrists so he could at least power a wheel chair under his own strength.

Whenever he could, he would wheel himself over to the children's ward with a focus to cheer up at least one sick child per day. He would call me each night to report on his success and to develop a strategy for the next day's mission. Charlie's only reward was witnessing a sick or crippled child stopping the tears long enough to laugh at his antics.

Charlie kept his newly-formed battle cry of cheering up one sick child a day going strong for months. He performed his mission like he was the Ruling King of Happiness and he had to defend his empire against the villains of sorrow. He soon realized, by cheering up the sick children, he was also picking up his own spirits. He was able to keep focusing on his own rehabilitation by keeping his task at hand, to help others to the best of his ability. Because Charlie stayed focused, his spirit successfully challenged his body until one day his spirit won out and his sickness surrendered. Charlie will never coast through life. He now counts his blessings, one step at a time.

Profile of Steel

Jim was a manager of a car dealership parts department. He started feeling as if something was not right with his health, so he visited a doctor. The diagnosis was not good. He was told he had cancer and would be lucky to live six more months.

Since he realized his days were numbered, he asked himself how he would live his last days on earth. He quit his job and asked himself how he would want to spend his last months on earth. His answer was flying planes, since he always wanted to be a pilot.

He first learned how to fly an ultra-light plane (a kite with a seat and a small motor attached), which is considered a dangerous hobby since the plane one flies is flimsy. His wife chastised him for doing something so dangerous, but he replied, "What's the difference, I'm dying anyway?"

As long as he kept living, he kept flying, eventually obtaining his pilot's license so he could spend his last days flying a plane; the only problem was that three years passed, and he was still flying. After he outlived his doctor's prognosis, further exams revealed that the cancer went into submission. Jim is now flying planes for a Fortune 500 Company and enjoying life to its fullest.

Can peace of mind be a possible cure for cancer?

Dialogue of Steel

Jim's Dialogue of Mush: *My days are numbered. I might as well just sit around and wait to die.*

Jim's Dialogue of Steel: *Everybody's days are numbered. Maybe I have been dead all along so now is the time for me to live, while I still have some time left.*

Jim's DOM: *I never had a chance to get what I wanted from life.*

Jim's DOS: *While I am still alive, I am going to start getting from life what I want, and I am going to start right now.*

Jim's DOM: *But I don't have time to get what I want from life. I am dying.*

Jim's DOS: *The problem here is not that I am dying. It's that I have not been living.*

Jim's DOM: *Some of the things I want to accomplish in my life may be considered foolish.*

Jim's DOS: *Maybe my life has not been foolish enough. Now I am going to fly.*

Create some new and exciting goals for yourself and start to make plans to achieve them. Commit yourself; do not just wish you could achieve your goals. Jim realized he was not living life due to a catastrophe happening; he was diagnosed with cancer. Do not wait for such an occurrence to wake you up. Wake yourself up on your own.

Nuts And Bolts From *Nerves of Steel* - Floor Five
How To Stop, Walk, and Then Run In Order To Avoid Coasting

You should now be focusing on your daily actions, achieving newly-found goals, recreating yourself, and figuring out what you want to do for the rest of your life. Spend your time more wisely instead of wasting it. You are only given 24 hours in a day, or 168 hours in a week.

The next time you tell yourself, "I'm not smart enough to tackle that project," or "I'm not qualified enough to interview for that management position," or "I'm not good looking enough to ask that person out for a date," or "I'm too tired to exercise tonight," or some other similar "I'm" that may crop up in your thinking during the day, you must have an immediate response to stop your mind in its tracks before you get derailed.

Try to stay calm and listen to your inner voice when difficult circumstances arise. If astronaut Lowell could remain calm as his spaceship hurdled aimlessly through space, you can certainly remain calm if you accidentally bounce a check, discover a flat tire or a dead battery in your car, or get scolded for arriving at work ten minutes late.

If you live life half-heartedly, you will look back on your life at a time when it is too late, and wonder *"what if ?"* What if you would have done some things differently? Do those things you always wanted to do now, before it is too late.

PHASE TWO-LIVE YOUR PLAN

What good is the most-organized and thought-out plan if the plan is not put into action? In the first part of the life-improvement manual *Nerves of Steel*, you were given advice, techniques, and exercises which allowed you to stop, take a look at your life, and start walking toward your destiny. In order to really run toward your destiny, however, you need to implement your plan and stay on track.

The process of running toward your goals is all you need to be classified as a success. The actual achievement of a goal is not your gauge to success, because after that goal is achieved, you will simply move on to bigger and better goals. The real proof of success is your determination to set goals, the actual journey toward your goals, and your ability to stay on track and stay focused in your life-improvement journey. Phase Two of *Nerves of Steel* will help you take what you have already learned about planning your life and help you to now live out your plan.

FLOOR SIX
Don't Be A Feather In The Wind

"How old would you be if you didn't know how old you was?" -
Sachel Page, Negro League baseball player

Researcher Julian Rotter stated that the person who believes in internal reinforcements, rewards, and successes in life and is controlled by personal behavior has an internal focus of control. A person who is strongly influenced by outside demands of their environment, such as what others say or do, has an external focus of control. This concept is known as "Locus of Control" and is made up of people classified as internals, who control their own lives, and externals, who let others control their lives. This concept was touched on briefly in chapter one of this manual.

I was pretty much an undisciplined, unruly child. As a result, I was often sent to my grandmother who lived a few blocks away so she could "straighten me out," which was a challenge she always seemed to welcome. One morning, I walked into our kitchen and my father was crying. When I asked what was wrong, he stated that Grandma had leukemia and only had a week to ten days to live.

I rushed over to her house and found her playing the organ and singing hymns. I sat down next to her and said, "Dad said you're gonna die!"

She answered, "Who told him that?"

I told her the doctors said so. She snapped back, "They are not God so I'm not going anywhere until I'm ready to go."

She lived almost three more years. She did not allow a force outside of her to be her reality. She trusted her internal source much more. The day before Grandma died, she said, "Now I'm ready to go home."

How much control we have on our own lives is not exactly known, but it is a great deal more than most people think. Focus on the task in front of you instead of wasting valuable time and energy processing information such as being worried about changes in the stock market, or if someone is watching what you are doing, or worrying about what your teammates or coworkers are doing. You will instantly be performing at a higher level if you stop being so external and start becoming more internal.

Deion Sanders was playing baseball for the Cincinnati Reds when a fan started to jeer him. After the fan shouted remarks toward Deion, who, in turn, walked toward the fan, looked at him, and said, "God bless you."

During his tenure with the Reds, relief pitcher Rob Dibble commented that Deion was one of the nicest players in the locker room and would do anything to help his teammates. Dibble said the impression many fans have toward Deion Sanders is totally wrong. Dibble said that the flashy, outspoken football player that most fans identify with is not the baseball player that is a joy to have in the clubhouse. The fans' mean comments did not influence how Deion thought or felt because he is internal, not external.

Dibble also commented on another subject. He once mentioned that players complaining about officiating, the league, the rules, and other factors beyond their control will lose focus. He felt the most successful athletes were ones that concentrated on doing their job. He never mentioned the concept of internals and externals, but he articulated the concept perfectly with the examples he expanded upon.

Research has documented internal and external focus. Santamaria and Furst (1994) found that 38 elite runners were examined and their most successful races and least successful races were analyzed. The subjects concluded that their most successful races were run when they were focused and their least successful races were run when they let outside influences affect them.

In a similar study by Kerr and Gross (1977) elite gymnasts suffered from high levels of anxiety and low self-esteem when they lost their internal focus.

Live Life In The Zone

There is a state of mind referred to in athletics called "The Zone." When an athlete is completely lost in his own world of performing and is oblivious to outside factors, he often achieves at abnormally high levels of success. This phenomenon is often referred to as "being in the zone." The athlete's body is almost completely taken over by an internal force that helps the athlete respond to the situation by telling the athlete how to move, what to do, and where to go.

If you witnessed any athletic performances in the past which you considered magical, chances are you were watching an athlete who was competing "in the zone." There is no reason you cannot live each day in the zone. You do not have to be an athlete, or be competing in a competition to experience the zone.

Do not concern yourself with outside approval and your full internal energy will be released. If internal energy provides more motivation toward success than external energy, why are most people controlled more by external energy than internal energy? Because it is much easier to be external than internal. If you allow your life to be controlled by external forces more than internal forces, you do not have to think as much; therefore, you do not have to work as hard at living life.

If you focus on following your path as laid out by your internal voice, you are certain to be more motivated while walking or running toward your calling in life. Your performance will be enhanced, and your life will be much more worth living. Think internally, believe what you are telling yourself.

How Can I Do It Better?

When Pittsburgh Steeler quarterback Kordell Stewart played in college, his Colorado Buffalo team was facing Michigan in one of the biggest games in his college career. In the fourth quarter, Stewart dove over the goal line and then dropped the ball. One official signaled touchdown but another official waived him off and signaled fumble. When Stewart returned to the sidelines, his coach asked him, "Do you trust me?"

After Stewart responded yes, the coach said, "You are going to win this game and all the people watching are going to witness one of the greatest comebacks in college football history."

Kordell thought the coach was crazy but said, "I trust you, coach."

The Buffalo offense got the ball back, but with very little time left on the clock. Stewart completed a pass at the 50 yard line, but there were only 6 seconds left. On the last play of the game, Stewart threw a Hail-Mary pass toward the end zone and teammate Michael Westbrook caught it for a touchdown to defeat the Wolverines 27-26.

As Kordell ran off the field, his coach said, "See, I told you so."

Everyone makes mistakes, sometimes mistakes worse than fumbling a football. You have two options to consider when thinking about what to do when you make a mistake. First, you can consider yourself a failure and ask yourself why you are always doing something wrong. This line of internal dialogue can be immobilizing as you criticize yourself after every mistake you make. Eventually, you will be so tired of criticizing yourself that you will no longer take any chances or make any tough decisions because you will be afraid of the outcome.

Or second, you can say to yourself, "What I have done may be wrong, but I am not wrong." The second line of thinking allows you to recover so you can move forward and either correct any mistake you made or put your mistake in the past. You will also be less afraid to make a decision in the future.

Everyone makes mistakes. Mistakes help you to learn and grow. A fancier word for mistakes is experience. Mistakes do not have to mean the death of you. Mistakes can actually be beneficial to you in the future. If you learn from your mistakes, then you will be less likely to make similar errors in the future.

An IBM employee made a mistake in the earlier days of the company. The error ultimately cost the company four million dollars. Thomas Watson, the founder of IBM, called the employee into his office. The employee asked Watson if he should quit before he gets fired. Watson replied, "Fire you? I just gave you a four-million dollar education."

Life is sometimes painful, but life should not be based on pain-avoidance or self-judgment. Life should be about learning and becoming a stronger person. If you try to live life to its fullest, you will make mistakes. Simply contemplate on what happened, what you could have done to prevent it, concentrate on not making the same mistake the next time, and move on.

In the movie *The Edge*, actors Anthony Hopkins and Alex Baldwin become lost in the woods after their plane wrecked. Anthony Hopkins looks at Alex Baldwin in a defining moment of the movie when their very survival is being questioned and asks him, "Do you know why most men lost in the woods die?"

Alex Baldwin replied, "I don't know."

Anthony Hopkins answers, "Shame."

Men have so much shame about making the mistakes that caused them to be lost in the woods that they lose focus on the task at hand, which is survival. Many people attempt to perform, but they simultaneously destroy their performance by judging who they are instead of what they are doing. If something bad happens, these types of people consider themselves failures. Such beliefs rob you of time, energy, and focus.

The next time you make a mistake, so what? You only made a mistake. Do not define your existence by the mistakes you make. You are not the mistake. Contemplate on what happened, ask yourself what you learned and what you could have done differently, and remember for the next time. Focus on your journey in life and you will not have time to think about mistakes. Keep looking to your motivating factors and keep to your mission. Do what will bring you the things you have identified in your previous exercises. Keep asking yourself, "What is it that I really want?"

You will have a much easier time answering the question if you free your mind from past mistakes.

Listen For Something Larger Than You

A thirteen-year-old sprinter was preparing for an upcoming race because he wanted to win it with all his heart. He was no ordinary sprinter, however. He was preparing for the Special Olympics, track and field events conducted for challenged-children. The sprinter proudly took his position at the starting line. The gun sounded and the race began. As he and three other runners took off, his excitement caused his legs to go out of control and he fell, dashing his dreams of glory.

The other runners saw what happened to him and they all stopped in their tracks, returned, and picked up the fallen athlete. Then all four challenged runners joined arms and crossed the finish line together.

Compare the vision you had in your head of that true story to the vision you would have had if you were reading about an Olympic athlete sprinting down the track in search of a world record. Which story touched your heart? Most people would answer the story of the special athletes because there is something inside all of our souls that craves community. We all need each other.

A young boy was upset with his parents, so he ran away. He took two cans of root beer and two twinkies to last him until he got to the park. At that point, he was so hungry he sat down on a bench next to an elderly lady and started to eat one of his twinkies and drink a can of root beer. He offered the elderly lady the other twinkie without saying a word. The lady smiled at the boy and accepted the twinkie. He then gave the lady one of his cans of root beer. She gave the boy another huge smile and accepted the can of root beer. When he was done with his snack he decided it was best to return home. He got up and started to walk away but turned around and gave the elderly lady a hug. She smiled at him once again.

When the little boy returned home, his mother was fascinated by how happy he now seemed. She asked why and he answered, "I just met God in the park and She had the most beautiful smile I ever saw."

After the elderly lady from the park returned home, her son, who was visiting her at the time, asked her why she was so happy. She responded, "I just met God in the park and He is a lot younger than I thought He would be."

A roommate of mine years ago heard the doorbell ringing at our house and upon answering the door, saw a Girl Scout standing on his stoop. When she asked him if he wanted any cookies, he replied that he already had some cookies and did not want any more, even though this was not true. When I approached him about why he had lied about the cookies, he said he did not feel like buying any cookies and did not want to simply say, "no" to the Girl Scout, so he made something up. He later felt very bad about his decision.

*Years later, he was walking through the airport and saw a Girl Scout selling cookies with a friend of hers. He stopped at their booth and asked how many boxes she had left and how many boxes the other Girl Scout had left. He bought all their boxes of cookies. He felt good about giving a donation to the Girl Scouts but he felt **great** about himself.*

The Lost Art Of Communication

"A porch is the only reward you need after a long summer's day," said Shawn Sell in the *USA Today* newspaper.

Have you noticed that homes are not built with porches anymore? Many communities have even passed ordinances forbidding the building of front porches on new homes. This small little piece of Americana makes a huge statement about the loss of our communal spirit. Porches used to be the place that we would meet with our neighbor and sit with them on warm, summer evenings. The porch was a place we addressed our needs and interacted as a community. People no longer look forward to community anymore, only privacy. Front porches have been replaced with decks off the back of the house so the inhabitants can hide from the community.

We have gotten away from community for many reasons. Either we are too busy, too stressed, or too private. Have you ever spent some time with a friend or a spouse when you thought you shared in an excellent conversation? Spending time when you talk with another and you each feel understood and enhanced by the conversation can feel very satisfying. Consider sharing such conversation with family or friends the next time the opportunity arises. Make community a priority. Practice the art of good old-fashioned communication. Bring back the porch.

In today's fast-paced world of e-mails, faxes, pagers, cell phones, and similar high-tech communications gadgets, our society has lost the sense of community, diminishing an important portion of the art of communication. We have grown exponentially in the field of communicating with the help of technology but have gone backwards in connecting personally with our fellow man.

When was the last time you listened to a radio program (News or sports updates do not count.)? Many AM radio stations still broadcast old-time radio programs such as *The Shadow*, or *The Lone Ranger*. When you listen to a radio program, you have to actually use your mind to visualize what is happening.

This lost art of visualization disappeared along with the lost art of sending and receiving a handwritten letter. When was the last time you actually wrote a nice letter to someone (a real letter, handwritten, addressed, stamped, and mailed)? Can you even remember? Have you ever written a letter? When was the last time you received a letter (Post cards and occasion cards do not count.)? Write a letter to someone and suck up all the positive feelings afterwards.

Bring back the community, bring back little-used or completely forgotten forms of communication. The people who receive a real letter from you will not easily forget the time and effort you put forth in doing something considered arcane by today's standards. What if you sent out personal letters to your Christmas list this year instead of generic, store-bought Christmas cards? (If your list is extensive, even a personalized, self-written form letter will suffice.) You will receive just as much pleasure, if not more, by resurrecting the personal Christmas greetings as your recipients will.

The Joy Of Hearing Others

The ability to listen is waning. Listening does not take a great deal of hard work, so it is perplexing why people generally do not listen anymore. We just want to be heard, but we do not want to take the time to listen. A great deal of relationships are strained for the simple reason that one or both people in the relationship are not listening.

In order to be a good listener, you have to send a message to the person that you care who they are and what they have to say. If you do not listen, the other person will sense that you think you are more important than they are, whether you actually say anything negative or not. If you think to yourself that you care about the importance of the other person, you will innately listen to that person. If you make an honest effort to listen to others before you talk about yourself, you will find greater joy in the other person's conversation toward you.

Mother Theresa said, "There is no disease as bad as not being loved by someone."

Not being important enough to be heard and understood runs a close second. Do not spread any more disease. Listen, really listen to whomever you may be communicating with, and then worry about saying what you need to say. Mother Theresa also said, "Kindness has converted more people than zeal, science, or elegance."

Each day you communicate with someone and each kind action you show towards another converts you closer to the state of mind Mother Theresa expressed most of her life.

There are many reasons people do not listen well. If you think you are more important and your problems and concerns are more important than other people's concerns, then you will come across as being a lousy listener, which is the same as saying you do not care about the other person. If you want to dazzle or impact someone with your line of conversation, then you may simply ignore what the other person is answering back. While they are talking, you are trying to think what you are going to say next instead of listening. And nothing feels as uncaring to a person as being cutoff while talking because you simply must overrule their concerns with your own.

You may also have a problem listening if your mind is somewhere else. Blank out any concerns for the time being when you are talking with someone. At that given time when you are engaged in conversation, no matter how trivial, the other person is owed the respect of being heard. They are more important than the chores, homework, or errands you may be thinking of while you are talking. The next time you are engaged in conversation, remember this simple phrase, "Clear everything out of my head, and concentrate on this conversation." Focus on the sole goal of only hearing what is being said.

A marvelous opportunity awaits you at this juncture. Most people do not listen very well, or do not know how to listen. The door is opened wide for you to burst through. If you are the only one, or one of only a few people who are good listeners, the people you are giving your attention to will not forget how caring you seem towards them. You can outrun your competition hands-down, just by listening. You will be remembered as one who actually cares about people.

Proper listening is active. Proper listening can be hard work at times, because listening does not mean just sitting there and nodding your head. Good listening means becoming active in the other person's conversation, catching every word and letting the other person realize with unspoken words and body language that you truly care what they are saying and you consider that person important. You can positively transform yourself and others around you through active listening.

Act Interested, Not Interesting

One way of defining insanity is taking the exact same actions, but expecting different results. If you want a different reaction from your family or friends the next time you communicate with them, try actively listening to them. Do not be so eager to tell them about yourself or your problems. Listen to their problems or concerns with your undivided attention. Be genuine in wanting to know about others and show interest. You will be amazed how powerful such a simple act can be.

Basketball coach Rick Pitino, of the Louisville Cardinals, and former head coach of the Boston Celtics, Kentucky Wildcats, and Providence Friars, was discussing the art of college recruiting during a television interview. He sensed that, when he would tell the player about their team, the facilities, and the wonderful program, he was less successful on signing players than when he focused his recruiting visit on listening to what the recruit had to say, rather than doing all the talking. Pitino realized he did not have to dazzle the player with what he could offer, but rather his listening to the player made the player feel comfortable and that he cared about them.

You should develop the habit of listening during every conversation. Acting interested is not acting, because there is nothing phony about active listening. By listening to others, you will never need to say to others who you are and how much you care about people. Who would you rather spend time talking with, someone who cares enough about you to listen to you, or someone you sense could care less what you are talking about?

Have you ever been helped as much as when you simply needed to talk and someone listened? One reason listening is so effective to calm a hurting person is because a hallmark characteristic of being hurt is isolation. When you feel hurt, you may feel that nobody else in the world feels as bad as you do at that time. Isolation is a breeding ground for evil. If one cannot find another to help ease their pain, then evil will find them.

Carl Jung once said that the principle of evil was so strong that only two things could keep a person from either being its victim or its perpetrator, either a strong soul filled with spirit or a person involved in a warm, human community.

Listening is one reason the concept of group therapy such as Alcoholics Anonymous (and similar associations such as Narcotics Anonymous, Gamblers Anonymous, Overeaters Anonymous, etc.) is so successful, because listening is the basis for the concept of community. You were probably more help to a friend in need by just listening than if you actually gave advice. Who do you feel more comfortable confiding in during tough times, someone who will give you advice, or someone who will listen when you need to vent?

There is no better business tool than the art of listening. Many business people and sales people have become successful by listening to the customer and their needs instead of trying to talk too much and to push something down a potential customer's throat.

I recently had some home remodeling done but was not pleased with the end result. I vowed never to use this company again and even called the owner of the company to express my feelings. He was a very effective listener. He even said that he would have been upset himself if such work was performed at his house. I was not prepared for such a response, so I was softened instantly. Before our conversation was over, in which I did most of the talking and he did most of the listening, I not only asked him back to correct the problems, but I contracted him for additional work.

Many children feel isolated. The number one concern heard from young children when they visit with counselors is that they do not feel understood, only pinned down with lectures and criticism. These same children usually feel lost. Many parents lecture instead of engaging in a give-and-take process. A lecture is one-sided because the lecturer is doing most of the talking and little of the listening. Children often say, "My father and I had words last night, most of them his."

Even when lecturing appears to be effective, the effectiveness dissipates rapidly. Usually when a lecture begins, the disinterested recipient builds a barrier and does not really hear the lecture anyway. Parents lecture not only to their children, but to other people they have relationships with, such as the other spouse. Lecturing is easier than communicating, because lecturing takes less thought and less work. You do not have to listen if you are lecturing. You only have to talk.

I counseled a woman named Sandy who was suffering from

Hodgkins Disease. She called me at home one Sunday evening and asked if she could have one last counseling session with me. Her only concern was that she needed it soon and that I would have to make a house call this time because she was dying. I had counseled this woman for over three years so I felt close to her. I told her I would be there for her.

I arrived at her home the next day. As she spoke, I hung on her every word and listened to her like I never listened to anyone else before. I did not want to miss anything Sandy had to say because I had such an urge to demonstrate to her how important I thought she was. One of the things she said was that she did not want anyone to pray for her because she wanted to die. She asked me if I thought she was crazy. I said to her no but maybe everyone else isn't crazy enough. She laughed and said maybe I was right.

We cried, laughed, and felt joy together. When I left her house that day, I thought 100 different things, but the thought that I considered the most glaring was when I wondered why I did not listen to everybody the way I listened to Sandy. She died three days later.

Since then, I have been improving my own listening skills and attempting to show people that what they have to say is important to me. That was the last lesson I learned from Sandy.

Profile of Steel

Jim Haslett was always known as being tough and hard-nosed, both in his playing and coaching days. When he was growing up, he constantly competed against his brothers in basketball in his family's driveway. Haslett also played several other sports as a kid.

After playing high school football, he played football at the college level, attending Indiana University of Pennsylvania where he earned All-American status three years. Haslett gained enough experience and ability in college that he was able to move up to the professional ranks. He was a second-round draft choice for the Buffalo Bills of the National Football League. He earned defensive rookie of the year honors and was a pro bowl selection in 1980 and 1981.

Since football was Haslett's passion, when his playing days were over, he moved into the assistant coaching ranks. He coached the linebackers at the University of Buffalo and later served as their defensive coordinator. He later coached in the World League for the Sacramento Surge before becoming the linebacker coach with the Oakland Raiders.

When he arrived with the Pittsburgh Steelers as defensive coordinator in January, 1997, he was one of the youngest defensive coordinators in the NFL. He excelled at his position to the degree that he was then hired to be the head coach of the New Orleans Saints in 2000.

Even though he coaches like he played, hard-nosed, he does include one attribute in his overall coaching style that would not seem to fit the tough persona. He constantly walks around the Saints complex and talks to each athlete one on one. Each morning he jots down on a yellow index card a list of players he wants to talk to throughout the day. He not only talks to his personnel, who range from quarterback Jeff Blake to the equipment manager nicknamed "Chief," but he actively listens to each person.

The Saints have always been known as a lowly team, but Haslett used his toughness to turn the team around. The Saints won their division, advanced to the playoffs, and eliminated the defending Super Bowl Champion St. Louis Rams. Haslett earned NFL Coach of the Year Honors.

Haslett commented that he coached a lot less football than he thought he would have to coach that year, because he focused on coaching men.

Can toughness and caring go hand in hand? *Absolutely*.

Dialogue of Steel

Jim Haslett had a reputation of being tough, but tough can only go so far. Sooner or later, players will tune out coaches if they think their coaches are browbeating them. If a player feels a coach truly cares for him or her, then no amount of toughness a coach can display will turn off a player's attention.

Haslett's Dialogue of Mush: I have to work on developing the game of football with these players, or I will fail.

Haslett's Dialogue of Steel: If my players don't trust me, no amount of teaching will work.

Haslett's DOM: But what if I don't push them to work as hard as they can work?

Haslett's DOS: It is not possible to push anybody to be successful on a consistent basis. You have to make them want to push themselves.

Haslett's DOM: But these players have to learn how to perform at a level they never performed at before so I can be proud of them.

Haslett's DOS: This is not about me. This is about us and our team. I must let each member of the team know how important they are by asking them what their dreams are and how they are doing. If I respect them as individuals, they will trust me. If they trust me, they will listen to me.

Haslett's DOM: But the task of improving this football team is important.

Haslett's DOS: Each person is important. When people feel important, they begin to rise to the occasion and take on the task at hand with maximum effort.

As a leader, whether you are leading your family members, school children, clients, or employees, let people know by your ears, not by your mouth, that they are important to you. Then, you will be important to them.

If you wish to be ruler over many, be faithful when the amounts are small.

Nuts and Bolts From Nerves of Steel - Floor Six
Don't Be A Feather In The Wind

If you are just floating through life like a feather in the wind, you are not living life and realizing your full potential. You may not even be scratching the surface of what you are capable of achieving. You were not put on this earth to lie on the couch, drink beer and watch television. There is nothing wrong with doing that once in a while, but if you waste most of your time with useless activities, you are probably floating through life like a feather in the wind.

Live life in the zone. When you are at work, think about work. When you come home, no matter what happened at work, put it out of your mind and concentrate on your family. If you go on a vacation or even go to a movie or the park with your family, just relax and let all worries behind.

Our entire lives are nothing but communication; whether we are dealing with others or talking to ourselves, we are constantly communicating. There are not many forms of communication that are more impersonal than e-mail. Communicating is not simply passing back and forth words. Facial expressions, body language, and the way the words are said actually make up about 90 percent of communication, while words make up less than 10 percent of communication.

The next time you talk on the telephone, react as if you really care about the other person, actively listen to the other person and make them feel important. If you send e-mail, try to personalize it as much as you can. This may be a challenge, but you will have fun figuring out ideas you can use.

Bring back the art of communication and practice it as much as you can. Try to invent new ways of personal communication that you may not have considered before. Write a letter to someone and notice how you feel afterwards. Spend some time reading a book instead of always watching television or surfing the internet. You will feel rejuvenated when you communicate if you now practice communication like an art, rather than a necessity.

We all know people whom we consider good listeners and bad listeners. Think of people you have known in the past or know presently whom you consider bad listeners. Maybe one person always cuts you off when you try to talk, maybe another looks around and stares into space while you are talking.

Think of the people you know or did know whom you considered to be good communicators. Maybe you felt they were paying attention to everything you said, or maybe they always asked you how you were doing before they told you how they were doing.

What you have compiled is a list of traits of how to be a good listener and a good communicator versus how to be a bad listener or a bad communicator.

FLOOR SEVEN
Beware Your Voice Of Judgment

"Fear can keep us up all night long, but faith makes one fine pillow." - **Philip Gulley in *Hometown Tales***

Read the following statement out loud:
"I was going down the street and I said to myself, 'The parking meter might be expired.' "

The preceding sentence mentioned two people, "I" and "Myself." The "I" person was talking to the "Myself" person in an active dialogue. It may sound odd, but that is how you must consider internal dialogue or self-talk, as a separate person.

Removing Yourself From Yourself

If you ever watched a young child play with an imaginary playmate, you are watching two people playing, for all intensive purposes. You can hear the child talking to the playmate. How come you may have difficulty in imagining what the playmate is saying back to the child, but the child is certainly receiving answers back from the playmate?

Adults usually give up their imaginary playmates because they would probably be judged as crazy if they still engaged in conversation with imaginary people. But there is no reason why you cannot successfully carry on dialogue with your own mind. Make your mind your new imaginary friend and perhaps your mind will be much more friendly towards you. Why not have another person on your side as you begin to rid yourself of destructive behaviors and attitudes?

If you have ever seen the movie *Fried Green Tomatoes*, the

overweight, unhealthy housewife in the film created a presence to assist her in her recovery of being fully alive. She called the playmate Tawanda and would often listen to Tawanda when deciding what the best decision was to make. Although the decisions Tawanda told her to make were sometimes not the healthiest, they were usually better decisions than the housewife was making on her own. She had developed a constant dialogue with herself by instituting another presence.

If you remove yourself from yourself, you are much more likely to have a successful conversation about what is going on and how you must act.

When I give talks, I am also talking to myself behind the scenes about the audience. I am asking myself if it is time for an anecdote, or if the audience looks interested in the topic, or if I should lower or raise my voice, or speak faster or slower. I have a conversation between me and myself.

Have you ever removed yourself from yourself and observed yourself in your surroundings? The concept of removing yourself from yourself may sound strange to you, but it is easier than it sounds. If you are facing a dilemma and you simply step back for a few moments, analyze the situation, and then take action, you are removing yourself temporarily from yourself so you can figure out what direction to take. You can also think and act while being less nervous. You will have a better chance to focus on the task at hand and perform more successfully.

Controlling Your Behavior Using Internal Dialogue

The best way for you to develop discipline is through proper internal dialogue. Your Voice of Judgment, that voice in your head that always criticizes your actions or your being, needs to receive and understand the fact that you are not going to be controlled by poor self-dialogue. By engaging in self-treatment, you can be your own therapist. Consciously start to exercise your thoughts in new ways of thinking with the goal in mind of creating a new script or program. Your self-dialogue needs to be rigorous and constant because you are rehabilitating the mental muscle, perhaps a muscle that has become debilitated due to lack of proper use.

The key to internal dialogue is debating and challenging the unfocused sentences your Voice of Judgment shouts at you from time to time. By focusing, you can pursue the restructuring of your internal philosophies. Your goal of using internal dialogue is to recreate a new and improved powerful philosophy revolving around positive internal dialogue. You can achieve this using a three-step process.

First, pay attention to your Voice of Judgment. Listen to what your Voice of Judgment is telling you. Think about what you think about. (If this concept seems confusing to you, reread the previous section which mentions removing yourself from yourself. Both concepts are similar in nature.) You may be surprised what your mind tells you. Such examples may be, "I never get what I want," or "I deserve self-pity," or "Why can't I do anything right?" Alert yourself of these and similar internal questions that your Voice of Judgment may try to force down your throat. When such a thought pops into your mind, put an immediate stop to it by asking yourself what you are really telling yourself and why.

Homme (1965) believed thoughts triggered actions or habits. He also thought thoughts could be modified just like behavior is modified, so he devised ways to change our thinking.

Horan (1971) conducted studies based on the effects of Homme's motivational approaches in regards to patients who were trying to lose weight. His conclusions were to keep your good intentions at the forefront of your awareness unless your needs compel you to think about your major goals many times a day.

Next, by paying attention to your internal self-dialogue, you can then challenge groundless statements the Voice of Judgment shouts at you. When you are burdened with negative statements entering your mind, rebut them at all costs and figure out an alternative to answer back. An example would be if your Voice of Judgment tells you that you deserve self-pity because you have an unloving spouse, answer back to yourself that you can address the problem and get to the root of it instead of sulking about it.

And thirdly, you now know the techniques in order to change your focus and move on. If you dwell on an attribute after you have determined you were being irrational, the Voice of Judgement may start to mount another argument in its favor. Simply refocus on your motivating factors and stop the Voice of Judgment dead in its tracks from controlling your mind and your life.

RECAP: When your internal dialogue brings up negativity either by way of telling you negative statements or telling you to take negative or destructive actions,

First: Become aware what your Voice of Judgment is trying to do.

Second: Challenge the negative statements.

Third: Change your focus and move on in a more positive direction.

Fear

You may suffer from fears you have been carrying around for years, perhaps your entire life. Often, your fears are based on a tumultuous event that either happened or you believe to have happened. As a result, you keep telling yourself you should be terribly concerned about your fears and keep dwelling on the possibility that the fearsome event may reoccur. An event cannot cause fear. You cause the fear by how you interpret the event or circumstance. Even if a fearsome event was to reoccur, thinking about it and being fearful of it will not stop its reoccurrence.

Some people may have had traumatic experiences in their life. Such events cannot be discredited. If you have been traumatized, why not let the event go and move on with your life? You may be held back from living your life to its fullest because of fear. Fear can cloud your vision and sap precious energy from your reserves, disallowing you to give full effort to realize your goals and your dreams. Unfortunately, fear is one of the hardest personal attributes to rid ourselves of because it can become so rooted in our subconscious.

There are many types of fears, including the fear of being rejected, of being alone, of not being loved by anyone, of various phobias, of what others might think, and of dying. The only way to conquer any fear is through your thinking, because it is your thinking that is causing the fears in the first place. The fear that an event or occurrence might happen is, in some cases, more immobilizing than the actual occurrence. Many people suffer from anxiety and panic attacks but cause more suffering to themselves from worrying about whether the panic attack will occur.

Rose Ann was a bright, attractive surgeon. As a little girl, she always aspired to be a surgeon. One night when she was fifteen, her parents were not home so she was alone watching television.

Three neighborhood boys came to her house and called her from outside a window. She reluctantly went outside and was attacked. Two of the boys held her down and the third ripped her clothes off. They stopped short of raping her, but the vile experience immobilized her for years.

She lived in constant fear of being raped and was resentful of all males. She carried in the back of her mind the fear that next time the rapist would finish the act. It took her fifteen years to finally accept what had happened, get over it, and move on with her life. The event was not immobilizing her later in life. She was being tortured by her thoughts and fears about the event. She was finally able to move on and put the past behind her after she controlled her thoughts and realized how much her anxieties were getting in the way of her present and future life.

The Fearsome Fivesome

Many fears appear in people's Voices of Judgment. The following is a list of five of the most popular fears rooted in many people's minds. Listed after each popular fear is a usable rebuttal which will give you some ammunition to fight back against your Voices of Judgment whenever these common fears surface in your mind. You may face other fears as well, some on a daily basis. If a fear arises that is not on this list, use what you have learned to design your own rebuttal.

FEAR NUMBER ONE: The Awful Past Will Repeat Itself

It is common for people to insist on relating their lack of achievements to the their past. The past can range from twenty minutes ago to twenty years ago, it does not matter. Past experiences can be as devastating as being abandoned by one or both parents to as minor as being called a name by someone. If you suffer from this fear, do not let the past affect your adulthood. If your Voice of Judgment is telling you that you deserve to feel sorry for yourself, you are only recreating a sad drama to define your life.

If you blame your family for raising you wrong, you are also defining your present through what you perceive to be an unsuccessful childhood. If you think you will fail in your present job or relationship because you have failed in similar situations in the past, you are once again defining the present through the past. Your mind does not have to work that way.

Rebuttal to Fear Number One: Do Not Let "What Was" Influence "What Is"

Realize that what happened in the past cannot be changed and engage in creating a positive life for yourself in the present. The more you recreate any negativity of the past in your mind, the more you are letting yourself be immobilized. No matter how trivial or how traumatic past experiences may have been, there is someone, somewhere who has endured the same pains and who has looked back on their lives by completely accepting their past and has since successfully continued their lives.

Recently, a man told a counselor that his wife wanted to leave him. The man felt there was no longer a reason to live. The counselor handed the man a notebook and a piece of paper. He told the man to compare the notebook with the rest of his life and the pen was his day-to-day thoughts and actions. He had two choices, fill up the notebook with morbidity and hopelessness, or fill up the notebook with hope and happiness. Either choice was solely up to him.

If you are having problems dealing with the past, tell yourself to focus on the now. Tell yourself to "Live in the today," or "Start new," or "Be in the now, not in the then." Focus on your goals, your dreams, and your desires. If something does not go your way, do not say to yourself, "Here we go again." You are only drumming up your Voice of Judgment, who will oblige you with negative self-talk at the drop of a hat. Your life of the present deserves its own fresh start.

FEAR NUMBER TWO: I Am Going To Be Rejected

The feeling of needing approval from others is highly addictive. If you feel the need for everyone to like you or to accept 100 percent of your actions, you are asking for failure. If someone else disapproves of your action(s), do not take that to mean that you are disapproved of as a person. What someone else thinks about you should be unrelated to how you feel about yourself. Other people's opinion of you or your actions should not be your concern, so do not let it concern you.

When someone disagrees with you, it can be an uncomfortable feeling. Do not make other's opinions of you needs-based, but rather wants-based. For example, you need water, air, food, rest, but you may want a chocolate sundae. In other words, it is nice to be agreed with or approved of, but it is not necessary.

Rebuttal to Fear Number Two: I Can't Please Everyone; I Can Only Live My Life

Abraham Lincoln said, "You can fool some of the people all of the time, and all of the people some of the time, but you can't fool all of the people all of the time."

This quote was referring to deceit, but the same concept can be said about rejection. You can please some of the people all of the time, and all of the people some of the time, but you can't please all of the people all of the time. So do not waste any time or energy trying to please everybody all of the time, a feat that cannot be accomplished.

You are going to be rejected from time to time. Accept that fact and live your life the way you see fit. If you get upset or worry over what others think about you, you are admitting to yourself that you place more importance on what others think of you versus what you think of yourself. You do not want to place a great deal of value on another person's opinion because only *you* have experienced your life and only you know what you are capable of doing. Only *you* know what dreams, goals, and aspirations are in your mind, so how can you place so much importance on what others think?

You cannot stop others judging you any more than you can guard against mosquitoes while walking through a swamp. You may stop all the mosquitoes from biting you (maybe), but you have little chance of doing anything else. Do not waste valuable time and energy wondering about what others may think of you because you could be using the same time to think more positive thoughts and take more positive actions.

If you concentrate too much on what others think, tell yourself, "I can only live my mission and I can only do it for me," or I can only live the way I believe is best for me." Keep your momentum moving forward toward your own rainbow, not towards someone else's rainbow.

FEAR NUMBER THREE: The Fear Of Not Being Perfect

You may have a false notion that everyone loves perfection. You may have heard the sayings that strive for perfection, especially in corporate America. We have all been conditioned to strive for perfection, but being perfect is not always mandatory for surviving.

Most people who have seen the movie *E.T.* thought the movie was touching. They fell in love with the *E.T.* character, and felt choked-up before the movie ended. One reason *E.T.* was so lovable was due to his being so imperfect. Have you ever seen the movie *Elephant Man*? When he cried out that he was not an animal, were you not touched? The Elephant Man is another example of a character being loved even though he was as far away from being perfect as one can imagine.

A study was done involving the success rating of four people who walked into a room one-by-one, sat down, and were interviewed. A confident person calmly walked into the room, sat down, and scored high on the interview. Next, a person with confidence walked into the room, and before he sat down, he accidentally spilled some coffee on the desk of the person who was interviewing him. Next, a nervous person with no confidence walked into the interview and spilled coffee on the desk of the interviewee. Finally, a nervous person walked into the room and stumbled his way through the interview.

As you might have guessed, the nervous person who spilled coffee was ranked lower than the nervous person who did not spill any coffee, but, the confident person who spilled coffee was ranked higher than the confident person who did not spill coffee. The point is that if you are confident and secure with your own behavior, being imperfect at times may actually be better than being perfect.

You should strive to be your best, but if you make a mistake once in a while, so what? Do not paralyze yourself with worry that you were not perfect in your behavior. Your worth is not always equal to your performance. Picasso did not worry after every brush stroke if he was being perfect. Your life can be a masterpiece too, if you take that big rock off your shoulders that is pressing down on you and demanding you to be perfect.

Rebuttal To Fear Number Three: Focus On The Task Without Regard To Being Perfect

Great performers, whether in music, athletics, or another form of entertainment, often say their mind was blank while they were concentrating on giving the best performance they could. They are not judging their performance as they perform, only concentrating on doing their best and letting the performance come out on its own. You can live your life the same way. Give your best and whatever the result is, do not paralyze yourself wondering if you were perfect or not. Every great creator and performer was far from being perfect, whether it was Thomas Edison, Babe Ruth, or the Beetles.

If you worry too much about being perfect, tell yourself, "I must focus on the task in front of me and whatever happens, happens," or "I will not judge my actions so harshly," or "I must paint my canvas but not worry about my brush strokes." We are not flawless, so why should you think everything you do should be flawless?

FEAR NUMBER FOUR: The Fear Of Not Having Power

Many people suffer due to hurtful acts on a small and large scale committed by people seeking power. When one seeks power, they may commit hurtful acts ranging from petty, such as a child throwing a temper tantrum, to disastrous, such as a person shooting, stabbing, or even killing another. Power can mean to control, but also to influence. Many power-mongers seek to control, but do not realize the ability to influence is real power. Al Capone controlled people. Ghandi influenced people. Both people had power, but who contributed more to society?

If you feel you are powerless, seek to influence, not to control, and you will truly be a powerful person.

Rebuttal To Fear Number Four: You Can Be Powerful If You Know Where To Find It

A man who once worked for a major company walked around placing stickers on people's desk when they did something special. The sticker read "D.W.D," which stood for "Damn-Well Done." When he passed by, people were influenced to perform their best. When he retired, the company organized a retirement party and it was the largest crowd a company-retirement party ever attracted. During the party, everybody chanted, "D.W.D." This man had power.

Throughout history there were people who had power and there were people who were powerful. If you care about people and develop the skill to make people feel good about themselves or to understand people, you will be powerful.

The most truly powerful being on earth commanded no one, yet he influenced the world forever in time. He gave no orders, yet he understood people, helped people, and influenced people to behave positively toward their fellow man instead of behaving like barbarians.

If you worry about not having any power, tell yourself, "Listen to others and focus on what they are saying and what they may need from me," or "Help others and I will be powerful," or "Care about them because they are hurting," or "I am a peacemaker." After helping someone or caring for someone, sense the feeling you have in yourself. That feeling radiates toward others as power.

FEAR NUMBER FIVE: The Fear Of Life Not Going The Way You Want It To Go

This fear can be considered two-fold, worrying about what will happen in the future and wondering why certain things happened in the past. Life can be difficult and challenging at times.
More times than not, life will not go the way you want it to go. But every thing happens for a reason. Sometimes people get sidetracked during their life's journey and find themselves somewhere else, much to their benefit.

After journalist Hugh Downs retired from the ABC News show *20/20*, he wrote a musical piece which was performed by world-renowned cellist YoYo Ma. Downs stated that his heart was always in music, but he got sidetracked along the way and became a journalist, a profession he ultimately dedicated his life in doing. Downs' life did not go exactly as he thought it would when he was growing up and becoming interested in music. His life did not turn out bad, however. He became successful and well-respected in the field of journalism, an entirely different field than music.

If your day does not go the way you planned, so what? Maybe that is for the better. Do not waste time and energy worrying about if your day or your life will go as planned and then lament when things do not go as planned.

When I accomplished the last feat of obtaining my doctorate, which was to defend my paper in front of a panel, I wondered why I did not hear any bands playing as I walked out of the room. So I decided to call my parents to hear their reaction that I was now a doctor. I called home and my father picked up the phone. I said, "Dad, this is your son, Dr. Elko." His reply was "Call back later, your mother is getting her hair fixed." As I heard the phone hang up in my ear, I was aghast. Then someone in the office walked by me and said, "Hello, Kevin." I suddenly came down off my cloud and thought, "Oh, my God, I am still Kevin." I soon realized who was being crazy, and it was not my father, but rather me for having such built-up expectations.

Life will be challenging at times, accept that fact and you will lose less sleep over worrying about whether life is going your way or not. The thought of raising children for people considering being parents is a prime example of life maybe not going the way you want it. After all, losing sleep, spending countless hours at the doctors' offices and hospitals, changing thousands of diapers, spending thousands or hundreds of thousands of dollars on a child, and then seeing them seek a psychotherapist to help heal all the scars the parents supposedly caused are usually not the first thoughts of people planning to have children. Yet a great deal of people happily become parents and most say becoming a parent is a wonderful experience.

If you are having a stressful day and you tell yourself that nothing is going right, you are needlessly increasing your stress level even more. Stop being so demanding on yourself by requiring that everything must always go as planned.

Lazarus and Folkman (1984) concluded through their studies that the little daily hassles, rather than the major life events, bother us the most and cause mental and physical problems.

Rebuttal To Fear Number Five: Align Your Expectations With Reality

When you really analyze your life, all you really have is your time and your energy. Everything else is a result or a by-product of how wisely you use your time and how you expend your energy. Researcher Abraham Maslow once stated that people are over-developed survivors and under-developed achievers, which means people spend too much time wishing things were different. Quit wasting time and energy wishing things were different and you will have much more time and energy to spend on more meaningful and useful endeavors.

Whatever happens in your life, trust that it has happened to allow you to become a better person. By aligning your expectations with reality, you expect whatever happens to happen, and you will quit asking yourself, "Why?" and tell yourself, "What is the best way to handle this situation."

If you are worrying too much whether life will always go your way, or chastising yourself for past mistakes, tell yourself, "Whatever happens, happens," or "Whatever happened, happened," or ask "What is the best way to remain calm and address this situation?"

If something happens you must address, do something about. If you worry about future events, you are only placing excess demands on yourself, which will eat away at your ability to give all your time and energy to your tasks at hand.

Profile of Steel

Sam was concerned about his cousin Danny's drinking problem. Danny began drinking in the sixth grade. His addiction was at the point that it was now taking its toll on his wife and children. When Danny's health began deteriorating, his family was so conditioned to his drinking that they paid no attention.

Sam was also concerned about the rage Danny now exhibited. Anyone who approached Danny about his drinking problem caught an earful of abuse and was battered by Danny. Sam knew he had to do something because Danny was at the point where he would not live much longer in his present condition. So he approached Danny and his family and discussed the drinking problem.

Danny eventually checked in to a treatment program and was able to stay sober for over a year. His sobriety did not last, however, and the next time Danny succumbed to his addiction, it killed him. Sam spoke at Danny's funeral. He had wished he spoke up sooner, and maybe he could have saved Danny.

Have you ever wanted to approach a family member or a friend and discuss a serious matter with them, but were afraid because of how you thought they would react?

Dialogue of Steel

If Sam would have approached Danny earlier, maybe his life would have been saved. Maybe not. There is no way to tell. Sam, however, will be thinking for the rest of his life if maybe he could have saved Danny. Sam did eventually approach him, and because of that, Danny was able to live a sober life for over one year.

*Sam's **Dialogue of Mush:*** *If I approach Danny, he may not like it too much.*

*Sam's **Dialogue of Steel:*** *Danny is blinded by his addiction. I can't worry about the consequences because I know, deep down, the Danny that will lambast me is not the real Danny, but the evilness that has taken over Danny's soul.*

*Sam's **DOM:*** *But what if Danny blasts me like he does everybody else that approaches him about his drinking problem?*

*Sam's **DOS:*** *So what? If I can ultimately save Danny's life, the initial abuse would be worth it.*

*Sam's **DOM:*** *But what if I approach Danny and it does no good at all?*

*Sam's **DOS:*** *At least I have tried. Isn't his life worth at least taking the chance that I can save it?*

*Sam's **DOM:*** *Danny is too far gone. I can't do anything that can help him at this point.*

*Sam's **DOS:*** *But by intervening, I will have the peace of mind for the rest of my life that I tried.*

It is better to try something and fail, then to never try it and wonder what might have happened if you did try. You cannot go back and live life over. Your life will reach a point some day when you are no longer able to go for most of your life-long dreams, but are only able to ponder on what might have been, if. . .

Nuts And Bolts From Nerves Of Steel - Floor Seven
Beware of Your Voice of Judgment

If you let your Voice of Judgment rule your life, you are losing complete control of your ability to think clearly and act to the best of your ability. If you can tame your Voice of Judgment and use your self-talk to your advantage rather than to your disadvantage, you will be able to live a much fuller and more productive life. Use the three-step process, if necessary, to undo the effect of a negative Voice of Judgment.

- **Become aware of what your Voice Of Judgment is trying to do.**
- **Challenge all negative statements by changing your focus.**
- **Move toward a positive direction.**

There is never enough that can be said about conquering fear. Many authors, including Dale Carnegie, have written many books addressing how to conquer fear. Fear is probably the most deeply-rooted emotion in the human species, so fear is not going away any time soon. The best way to deal with fear is to face it.

Do you fear that bad experiences in the past will repeat themselves? Do you fear rejection? Do you worry about not being perfect? Do you worry about being powerless? Do you worry about life not going the way you want it? Do you have any other fears? We all have fears. The key is not to let fear cripple your life. Fear can be good at times when it keeps you from jumping in front of a moving car or jumping from a roof of a building. These are not examples of crippling fears. Fear of speaking in public or fear of rejection are examples of crippling or potential crippling fears.

According to Zimbardo (1973), a backwoods midwife had predicted that a woman's two sisters would die before their sixteenth and twenty-first birthdays and that she would die before her twenty-third birthday. All her predictions occurred just as she had predicted. Was the reason because she could foresee the future, or because the woman and her family took the predictions as truth and self-programmed themselves to react to the midwife's predictions?

Many times, your emotions, including fear, become programmed. Your problem becomes not just thinking negative thoughts, but your previous conditioning making it easier and easier to think those bad thoughts each time the opportunity presents itself. (More will be covered concerning this concept in the next chapter.) Have you ever smelled a certain perfume or cologne and thought about someone you know who wears a similar scent? Did you ever hear a certain old song and it reminded you of an old experience you once had pertaining to that song?

You can program yourself to conquer fear in a similar fashion. Pick one of your fears from your list. Now close your eyes and see yourself experiencing that fearful feeling. For example, if you have a fear of speaking in public, picture yourself about to get up to speak in front of a crowd and feel the fear building up. Tell yourself, "This may be hard, but I can do it," or "I may not like it, but I can stand it, and after time, I will like it." Feel more relaxed and focus on the process of addressing your fears. Now remove yourself from yourself and see yourself focusing and being more relaxed. What did you do, or what can you do to face your fears and conquer them? Maybe you observed yourself breathing calmer or relaxing your shoulders.

The next time you feel fear coming on, or your negative Voice of Judgment attempts to put fearful or negative thoughts in your mind, put the three-step process into action. Use your fear-conquering observations to plug into step three of the process, where you focus your attention on conquering the fear and moving on in a positive direction.

FLOOR EIGHT
What You Think Is What You Get

"Men are not disturbed by my things, but by the view they take of them." -**Epictitus**

About 2,000 years ago, Epictitus also taught that our thoughts can change our feelings and actions, so by modifying our thoughts, which may be easier than changing some behavior or having some experience, we can possibly change many things such as actions, emotions, and other thoughts.[1]

Many people have said after giving memorable performances that their mind was simply blank and they were thinking about nothing at all, almost as if something larger than them took over their bodies. They were concentrating on performing rather than judging themselves. There is nothing that hurts performance more than thinking about it, because thinking too much can clog your mind, rendering it useless to perform. When you let your mind go, the activity you have practiced for will naturally emerge without your having to judge what is good or bad about what you are doing. Then you can throw all your effort into your performance.

Thomas Edison once said, "Most of life's failures happen because people gave up when they were closer to success than they realized."

Did Edison critique and make adjustments? Yes. Did he judge? No. Every time he did not get the results he wanted, he just changed what he was doing to get different results, but he did not judge what he was doing. He just kept working at what he loved doing.

Judgment can also be nerve-wracking. A bad event or occurrence is not what upsets us, but rather we are affected by how we judge an occurrence. Since we are affected by the meaning we give to an event, judgment can discourage us and take the joy away from what we are doing. Even if you think you know what is going to happen, act like you do not. Let your mind go blank and your body will naturally take over.

When U.S. pilot Scott O'Grady's plane was shot down over Bosnia, he refused to judge his situation. Instead of thinking it was all over since he was shot down, he focused on survival, such as sending signals on the radio for help, or eating bugs and grass and drinking his own sweat to stay alive until he was rescued. If O'Grady would have judged, he would have immobilized himself and may have been doomed. He was rescued and made it back alive to the United States as a hero rather than as a corpse in a body bag. He mobilized all his faculties and sense and concentrated on survival in order to succeed.

Avoid the negative voice in your mind. You can be fully aware of that negative voice, but you do not have to listen to it. Throw yourself into what you are doing instead, act with intensity, and turn your activities into joyful experiences.

When the voice of destruction starts to speak, you must talk back. An example of your voice of destruction acting up is your mind telling you there is no way you can achieve a goal because you are not capable of performing an activity perfectly. Tell yourself to stay focused and just perform, everything will turn out fine.

I was explaining how I was one of the first counselors on the scene of the plane crash in Hopewell Township, a few miles from the Greater Pittsburgh International Airport. I counseled family members of the victims as they arrived on the site. After my talk, a Chicago business man approached me and said he had a past experience where his secretary was supposed to book him on a flight from Chicago to Pittsburgh. She got busy and called too late to get him on that flight, forcing him to take a later flight. He called her back and severely scolded her because he was not able to fly out of Chicago at the time he wanted to leave. He later found out the flight he wanted to be booked on was the ill-fated flight that crashed, leaving no survivors. He hasnever passed judgment on an individual or a situation since.

The Zones of Performance

In order to understand your performance better, familiarize yourself with the four performance zones. The first performance zone is called **The Low Zone With Judgment**.

When you perform in this zone, you have a low energy level because you judge too much. If you ask yourself what happened after a sub-par performance, you usually find out that you were thinking too much. As a result, you let your thoughts control your behavior and you performed in the Low Zone With Judgment.

There are also times when you perform poorly for no reason. This is called **The Low Zone With No Judgment**. Researchers have made many attempts to explain why this occurrence happens by conducting studies using bio-rhythms, brain waves, air pressure, and many other methods. There are no clear-cut explanations why some days you are simply not yourself. Maybe you did not get enough rest or exercise, or you are stressed about something.

The key is to move yourself out of this funk as soon as possible or you may slide into Low Zone With Judgment because you may start to consider yourself a failure just because you are having a bad day. If you relax and do not worry, but rather focus on your goals and your activities, you should get back on track as this zone, too, shall pass.

The state you find yourself in when everything seems to be going right and you are thinking good things is called **The High Zone With Reason**. You are performing in this zone when you get the promotion, make the sale, get the good grade in class, ask the person out on a date and they say yes. You have reasons to be happy during these pleasurable moments. You deserve to be happy. This zone is full of the believers, the positive-thinkers, the people who consider themselves successful.

There is nothing wrong with being in this zone, but beware of allowing judgment to sink in. If you allow judgment, some of your mental capacity is consumed when you could be using it to contribute to your peak performance. So being in **The High Zone With Reason** is much better than being in any of the low zones.

If you reach the state where you no longer have to convince yourself to operate at peak performance, and it just happens, then you are performing in **The High Zone With No Reason**. This is the state you achieve when you feel good for no reason, or you perform at a high level almost unconsciously. In **High Zone With No Reason**, your mind is almost in a meditative state. The key element in this state is that you are not judging, either good or bad. Your mind is quiet and detached. You surrender to all judgment and become lost in the activity as it unfolds in front of you.

Obtaining **High Zone With No Reason** is difficult at times, especially when you are forced to start from one of the low zones. The more judgment you release, the closer you will become to performing at a **High Zone With No Reason**. Do not even classify the situation you are in as being good, bad, or indifferent. Just tell yourself that the situation you are facing, or the activity you areabout to embark on, is what it is, and no more or less.

During the 1998-99 Division I college basketball season, the University of Pittsburgh Panthers hosted the heavily-favored, undefeated Connecticut Huskies. The crowd sensed an emotion coming from the Panthers which began with the body language of the Pittsburgh players when they were introduced before hand. They came to play and played the entire game in the High Zone With No Reason. The Panthers found themselves winning the game with less than one minute remaining on the clock.

But judgment crept in and the team slid into Low Zone With Reason, as the players wondered to themselves if they would be able to win such a big game. A nine-point Panther lead with a little more than one minute to go shrunk to a one-point lead with less than ten seconds remaining as the Panthers committed consecutive turnovers and the Huskies converted quick two and three-point baskets at the other end of the floor. The star Panther, point guard Vonteego Cummings, who went on to be a first round NBA draft pick, threw the ball away with nine seconds left, giving the Huskies a chance for a winning basket, which they converted with two seconds remaining to steal a victory from the jaws of defeat.

Many great performers are able to empty their minds as they perform, allowing themselves to perform at peak levels without even having to think about competing. Michael Jordan has practiced meditation and yoga to enhance his mind to the level where he can perform at a top level without having to think about performing.

If you clear your mind and not dwell on possible consequences of your actions, your body will be able to take over and perform. You can still experience sorrow, disappointment, or anger. We are only human, after all. If you do not allow such negative feelings to distract or even immobilize you, then the fearful thoughts will pass and you can effortlessly re-engage yourself in your task or activity.

Do not allow yourself to be motivated by the approval of others. Do not allow yourself to be hindered by your own self-judgment. The less you judge, the more you can concentrate on performing at a **High Zone With Reason**, and eventually, you will find yourself performing at a **High Zone With No Reason**. You may have already performed at this level in the past but just did not realize what was happening. Have you ever done something you never thought you could, and then looked back and wondered how you achieved such a feat? That is an example of performing at a **High Zone With No Reason**.

The Development of Good Habits

Do you remember the first time you ate a piece of chocolate? You probably decided to take the wrapper off the chocolate, place the candy in your mouth and chew. The pleasure you received when you began to chew the luscious morsel probably made you think that you wanted another piece. The step-by-step process you engaged in was recorded in your mind.

You may have been conscious of this process the first few times you ever ate a piece of chocolate, but it probably did not take you long to be able to spot a piece of chocolate and already have it in your mouth before you even realized that you first peeled off the wrapper. The first time you ate a piece of chocolate, you formed a path in your mind similar to walking on freshly-laid snow. Each time you ate a piece of chocolate, the process became more familiar in your mind, just as a path in the snow would become more worn as you walked across it many times.

Each time you decide to act or react to a situation a certain way, you are wearing a path in the subconscious region of your brain, making it easier to walk that path when the situation arises again. As you repeat a behavior, the nerve connectors in your brain become more efficient and process the impulse with greater speed. In time, if a process is repeated enough, a particular activity will be beaten down in your brain similar to a path developing into a four-lane highway.

When you pick up your telephone and punch in a familiar number, have you noticed that your fingers know where the button is even before your mind has to tell you what numbers to punch in? Calling a familiar number is an example of a pathway that has been worn down in your brain. If you have repeated a destructive behavior over and over, it is just as easy for your brain to tell your body to keep repeating the hazardous behaviors.

Why do ninety to ninety-five percent of people who diet fail miserably? Even though dieters may be trying to eat differently or exercise more (some for the first time in their lives), there are still too many pathways in their brain that were formed by bad habits. If you have ever started a diet and almost unconsciously walked to the refrigerator and reached for a sweet snack, you are a victim of a pathway to the refrigerator that was worn down over time and is embossed in your brain. Unless you destroy the pathways of destructive behavior before you start dieting, your diet does not stand a chance. You cannot fight your body and your mind, no matter how much willpower you think you may have.

During Horan's diet study (1971), the dieters who thought about the consequences of being overweight as a motivator were the most successful in losing the weight. His study broke down the resultants into four groups. Group one members received no treatment. Group two members were given a 1,000 calorie diet to follow. Group three members were asked to create one positive and one negative affirmation which were associated to helping them lose the weight. For example, a positive affirmation may be repeating the advantages of better looks if the weight was lost and a negative affirmation may be poorer health if the weight was not lost. Group four members were asked to create one positive and one negative affirmation and link the affirmation to a daily task, such as repeating the affirmations every time a glass of water was drunk throughout the day.

The study results showed that only five percent of the group one members lost at least one pound or more per week. Twenty percent of the group two members lost one pound or more per week, and twenty-one percent of the group three members lost at least one pound per week. The group four members, however, showed an astonishing fifty-two percent success rate in losing at least one pound or more per week.

By linking the affirmations to a daily task, the successful dieters were constantly reinforcing their goal and re-training their brain to keep down the negative Voice of Judgment, who may have in the past said, "Let's make a beeline for the refrigerator!" The dieters were now saying throughout the day to themselves that if they lose the weight they will be better looking and will be healthier, which was a strong enough force to overcome their compulsions to overeat.

The Breaking Of Bad Habits

First, when you are about to perform an action inconsistent with your goals, in order to build up your nerves of steel, you have to recognize that you are about to walk down the same pathway of destruction. Quickly tell yourself to stop in your tracks. This simple technique will at least temporarily hold you back, even if it is for a few seconds, that will be helpful. Former NBA basketball all-star Charles Barkley developed a technique where he wore rubber bands around his wrists and when he was about to think something destructive, he would snap the rubber band to remind himself that he is about to embark on a pathway he does not want to go down.

The next step is to begin a new neurological pathway. When you are about to walk down the destructive path, picture yourself taking the fork in the road, and engaging in a positive behavior instead. If no fork existed, and you never took that particular pathway, you must now start one. Perhaps you never reached for the grapefruit juice in the refrigerator and instead always grabbed a Coke. If you decide to start a diet, or just a healthier lifestyle, for example, you may have to start a new fork in the forest where you find yourself having to construct some new pathways.

The first time you start down any new pathway, the going may be tough. If you have not engaged in a particular positive action for years, or decades, you may have to uncover an old path that is so grown over that you need a machete to cut through all the weeds and brush before you are able to navigate the route. An action may feel strange and difficult at first, but the more the path get sworn down, the easier it will be to walk down the path in the future.

By training yourself to calm down your negative impulses, you can give your mind and body a fighting chance to act on your best behalf instead of acting on our worst behalf. Of course, an important key to this process is recognizing that a bad situation or circumstance is about to arise. Change can immediately take place if you notice the moment adversity strikes. Noticing adversity allows you to gauge and strengthen your response.

Profile of Steel

Karen was an investment broker who was performing at an average level. She had suffered early in life from parents who constantly scolded her. She was also recovering from a recently-failed marriage. Maybe these events were shaping her attitudes and her present performance.

Karen was living in the "low zone with judgment." She questioned every move she was about to make, and ultimately, did not take a great deal of action because of her self-doubt. She refused to act on great opportunities. Before Karen would act, whether it was making a phone call or scheduling an appointment, she would wonder what would happen if she failed, so in most cases, she took no action.

She was *so* afraid of rejection that she failed to call someone qualified as a good lead because the individual was worth over fifty million dollars and was about to invest at least one-million dollars. Karen was then coached to repeat to herself two phrases, "Trust," and "No Judgment." She began silently repeating these phrases as she was about to take action. It worked. She found herself taking more action than she had ever taken in the past. As a result, she surpassed her sales goals by finding more investors and closing more sales.

She quit judging others' actions as well as others' reactions toward her. She no longer took other people's actions to be personal. By thinking stronger, Karen was able to battle through any past issues or attitudes that were previously affecting her performance and her life.

Have you ever wanted to take action, but were frozen in your tracks because you were concerned with the consequences?

Dialogue of Steel

If Karen would have continued listening to her negative self-talk, and worrying about what might happen if she took certain actions, she may have never become successful in her career and would have been penalizing her overall life as well.

*Karen's **Dialogue of Mush:** If I call this potential investor, I might be rejected.*

*Karen's **Dialogue of Steel:** If I tell myself, no judgment, and trust my abilities, I can then focus on the task at hand and contact enough potential investors that I will surpass my goals.*

*Karen's **DOM:** But why would an investor want to deal with me rather than a man, or someone older?*

*Karen's **DOS:** How could I possibly know who an investor would rather be dealing with?*

*Karen's **DOM:** I still feel like I will be rejected.*

*Karen's **DOS:** It is not me that is being rejected if an investor chooses not to invest in my suggestion. I should not take a rejection of the investment tool as a personal rejection of myself.*

*Karen's **DOM:** Won't I feel awful and terrible after being rejected?*

*Karen's **DOS:** I may feel uncomfortable, but the more I trust and the more I pass no judgment, the smaller the uncomfortable feeling will be.*

The biggest thief in your life is the thoughts and actions that steal your promises and your dreams. Do not judge an event before it occurs. Trust in your abilities and your intuition, not in your negative expectations or possible consequences.

Nuts And Bolts From Nerves Of Steel - Floor Eight
What You Think Is What You Get

You are a product of what you think, whether you fully realize the concept or not. The less you pay attention to your negative voice inside of your mind, and the more you act according to your positive voice inside of your mind, the better chance you have to positively transform your life. That is a simple statement, but not a simple task. Our brains have been conditioned for millions of years with certain traits and functions that may be a detriment to us now, rather than an asset.

Any activity you perform throughout your day, you are traversing in one of the following zones:
- **Low Zone With Judgment**
- **Low Zone With No Judgment**
- **High Zone With Reason**
- **High Zone With No Reason**

When you are performing at your peak, you are in a High Zone with No Reason, or simply called "The Zone" for short. Obtaining this state is not easy, but it becomes more possible as you develop nerves of steel.

Habits are developed as a result of repeating behavior. We all have good habits and bad habits. We want to at least leave the good habits alone and maybe even reinforce them, because they are positive and productive aspects of our lives. How many bad habits do you feel are currently victimizing you in some way? Maybe you swear too much or you bite your fingernails. Maybe you have a bad temper or you overeat at times.

How many of your bad habits are you guilty of performing on a daily basis, or even many times daily? Do you feel any of these habits are hindering your life, or are there any bad habits you would like to correct?

If a sensation occurs when you want to pick up your old destructive ways, and these sensations will happen frequently, remember to tell yourself to STOP right away. Actually picture in your mind of coming to a fork in a jungle and taking the opposite route instead of the destructive route. You will find yourself taking the positive path more and more often over the negative path until the positive path becomes worn down and the negative path becomes overgrown with weeds.

THE PENTHOUSE
Forgiveness, The Ultimate Strategy

Good to forgive; best to forget! Living we fret; Dying, we live.
- R. Browning, La Saisiaz: Dedication

Some years ago, the Pope appeared on the cover of *Time* magazine. He was pictured sitting in a jail cell with the person who shot him and attempted to end his life. This picture brought puzzlement to many who saw the cover. Immediate questions came to mind. Even though he is a devout man, does he realize what this individual tried to do to him? He aimed a gun and fired it at the Pope with every intent to kill him. The Pope must have gone through extreme physical pain in addition to all the trauma and emotional pain that accompanies the experience of being shot, never feeling safe again, or the bullet possibly causing complications down the road.

Here is the Pope, however, showing fellowship to his assailant. Why? For what reason would the Pope decide to go through the trouble to visit this evil man? It would have been so much easier for the Pope to just put this man out of his mind forever and let him rot in jail where he belongs with out showing one iota of concern for the would-be assassin. Obviously, this is not what the Pope was thinking when he stepped into his assailant's jail cell.

The Pope knew that it was not his own responsibility for what happened to him. He was only living his life according to the Word of God, which he was inspired to do. And part of living his life according to God's word is to forgive, not only to forgive the deed, but to forgive the doer. The Pope chose not to forget about the incident and try to put it aside, but he actually made an effort to become emotionally attached with the man who tried to end his life.

Sachel Page, the great negro-league baseball player, could have enjoyed a marvelous professional baseball career. He was one of the greatest baseball players of all time. He was not permitted to play major league baseball when he was in the prime of his career, however, because negro baseball players were prohibited from playing professional baseball; they were restricted to the negro leagues. Paige once said, "I will never allow another man to shrink my soul by making me hate him."

Viktor Frankl was a victim of Nazi concentration camps. He lost his parents, his brother, and his wife in the concentration camps during World War II. In his book *Man's Search For Meaning* (1963), Frankl explains the differences of living and surviving and how he used his mind to conquer his captors rather than wasting time hating his potential murderers.

When you were hurt by someone in the past, did you mull your wounds over and over? For some reason, we seem to need to chew on that bone one more time, to go over and over the hurt along with the feelings that are justified. We may never realize that the bone of the feast is our own and it is us that is being chewed and consumed by the constant gnawing.

Perhaps the Pope knew he would be a double victim if he did not forgive, a victim once by a would-be assassin's bullet, and a victim a second time by being crippled from not forgiving his assailant. Anger and hostility are far more damaging in the long run than a maiming bullet. If you do not forgive, you risk suffering spiritual and psychological deterioration until you can free yourself from the shackles of hate that bond you. You may rarely be punished *for* your anger, but you will usually be punished much more *by* your anger.

Why We Hold Onto Our Anger

Contrary to how easy it may sound in writing, forgiveness is tough. Real forgiveness takes a great deal of energy and it is so much easier to just forget, or even forgive and forget. The Pope, however, did not simply forgive and forget. He actively sought out to forgive. You may question if it is fair for you to make the effort to forgive someone who hurt you, especially if your tormentor shows no sign of apology. The answer is that it is not fair. Forgiveness, however, is imperative for your own well-being. You will never free the shackles that bind you until you have forgiven.

Forgiveness is not a one-time fix-it, either. It is a process you will have to repeat over and over again. If you are feeling anger towards any past tormentors, it may take many times until you are emotionally liberated. You may simply be holding onto your anger because of the mental anguish involved in forgiving and forgiving until you have completely forgiven someone. Also, the process of forgiving takes place in stages, which is another reason the responsibility of forgiving is difficult.

The work of Elizabeth Kubler Ross had a powerful impact in the area of psycho-spiritual healing. She is a physician who had the courage to study dying patients. She found that people who were grieving their illness had the potential of going through five stages: denial, bargaining, anger, depression, and then only acceptance. In order for the dying patient to progress to the next stage, they had to work at flushing out the previous stage from their minds. Only by moving through all the stages did the dying patients reach acceptance, which is an exquisite place to be for someone suffering so much emotional, and probably physical pain.

The problem with going through the work that each of these stages requires is that, after moving to the next step, a dying patient may feel a little better, but may be moving farther from reality. For example, in some ways, denial is not as painful as anger, for in denial, we delude ourselves of the truth, therefore; we do not have to completely deal with the pain.

So the reward for working through the denial and finish bargaining is anger. After anger comes another emotion that feels worse than anger, depression. Many feel, why work through the anger when depression is what awaits?

The reason it is important to understand the five phases of a grieving person is because the process of forgiving is similar. Initially, you will go into denial, either pretending that an act committed against you either never occurred or was not that big of a deal, and the arduous process of forgiveness begins. After you work through your denial, you realize that everything is not okay, so you bargain with yourself. Anger then rises to the surface. You may feel by holding onto your anger, you are inflicting a degree of revenge toward your tormentor. Similar to a grieving person, you must work your way through all the stages until true forgiveness can occur.

The revenge you feel you are inflicting towards others you feel have hurt you in the past is only eating away at your soul. So you are suffering twice for the same appalling act, once when the act is committed, and again when you replay over and over in your mind both the act and your hate and anger. In many instances, the person you are showing hate towards does not even know you exist, or may know you, but rarely thinks of you. Why, therefore, should you waste time and energy thinking about that person? We are only deceiving ourselves by thinking we are inflicting any degree of revenge toward our past tormentors by holding onto hate and anger.

Suffering

Nobody knows the reason for the existence of pain. Our earthly plane of logic does not provide us with the faculty to understand why there are people suffering in this world. The fact of the matter is, however, that we all suffer at one time or another. Every major religion claims the existence of suffering and that suffering is not sacred. You are not the only person who has suffered at some time in the past, so be careful not to get caught up in the "whys" of suffering.

It is easy for you to think you were hurt because you were not important enough or not worthy enough. You may often process the hurt by telling yourself if you were more important or more powerful, your tormentors would not dare hurt you. The reality is that your value or worth, whether it be actual or perceived, has nothing to do with having pain inflicted on you.

Your tormentors were not aware of your needs. They were only aware of their own needs, importance, or worth. An injurious act inflicted upon you had nothing to do with you; it had to do with your tormentor, so put the thought out of your mind that in some way, you may be causing other people to inflict pain on you.

Forgiving Through Nerves Of Steel

The word disease means there is a lack of ease, a lack of flow, especially proper flow of energy. How can you perform properly if there is no flow? How can you perform when there is no ease? How can you love? How can you live? The answer is you cannot. Even if you think you are performing properly, you could be doing much better if you were free from the bonds of hate, free from the bonds of holding grudges, and free from the conjuring up of some imaginary revenge you feel you are inflicting on your personal enemies.

A friend of mine approached me and said his wife was having an affair with another man. He asked me what he should do and I said forgive her. I then asked him how his law practice was doing and he answered, how could he concentrate on his practice and his clients after what he just learned his wife was doing to him? I said, "That's right, so let it go, because why would you want to keep beating yourself up over and over? Wasn't once enough?

Letting Go

A young mother recently diagnosed with cancer was angry at her parents for sending her the message that her needs were not important. She was angry with her husband for being so insecure while it was she who needed him to be sympathetic towards her. She was angry that she had to go through a rigorous treatment program which included chemotherapy. She was angry at herself because she no longer could control even her own life. Finally, she was angry at God for creating an unfair world where people get sick.

After doing much work and preparation, this woman surrendered. She let go of all her anger, her need for her parents, her husband, the world, and even God. Her surrender was that she cannot control that which is, but can control how she responded to what happened to her. She learned to look back at the past and live today with courage. As a result, this woman displayed a peace that I never saw in her before, probably a peace that she never saw in herself before, for that matter. She tried to control all that was around her, but she lost. Since she could not control all that was around her, she surrendered to acceptance. And only by losing did she win.

The Nervous System Of Steel

Your nervous system consists of two main parts: the voluntary and involuntary nerves. The voluntary nerves direct the movement of the limbs, head, and trunk. You control this system, theoretically, as you wish; therefore, the name voluntary.

The involuntary nerves are the endocrine glands that govern and regulate the normal functions of the body, including our body's reaction to stress. The involuntary nerves act like a highway, carrying messages from the brain to the internal organs, such as the heart, lungs, etc. Unlike the voluntary nerves, the involuntary nerves are not under your direct control, but they are influenced by your thoughts. For example, when you worry that something bad might happen, or you keep hateful thoughts in your mind aimed toward people you feel have hurt you in the past, rather than stay focused on the process of achieving your goals, your pupils may dilate, your heart may race, and your palms may become sweaty. You do not consciously react this way, but you have the power to stop these and other derogatory reactions, by changing the way you think.

Nerves Of Steel, A Factory That Cannot Be Shut Down

This entire book is based on changing the way you think. Developing nerves of steel means you are living life on all cylinders and are thinking the right things, thus doing the right things in order. Just as there is no destination in life, only a never-ending journey, there is no closing the book on nerves of steel. You cannot read this manual once and master all the *Nerves of Steel* principles just like you cannot exercise once and be healthy for the rest of your life.

Profile of Steel

Larry always wanted to be a head football coach. He paid his dues for years by performing to the best of his abilities in assistant coaching and coordinator roles. He was successful in all his previous appointments. One day, Larry's lifelong dream became a reality. He was hired as a head football coach.

Larry brought respect immediately to the program. The team performed at high levels on and off the field and won the conference. The community loved Larry, and many players and staff members loved Larry.

During his second year, the team did not win the conference. They did come in second place, however, which was good enough to make the playoffs, but apparently was not good enough. A few players, including the quarterback, approached the athletic director and criticized the system that Larry installed. Certain staff members and faculty played their political games and criticized Larry as well.

The athletic director joined in the lynching and fired Larry. When Larry was approached by the media the following day, he was obviously bitter for what he felt was unfair. He even shed a few tears. After he spent that evening talking with his wife, he came to the conclusion that everything happens for a reason, and maybe he would be better off in another position anyway.

When a friend called him to console him, Larry responded not by being bitter toward the people he thought wronged him, but by saying that the good Lord decided his job was done there, and that it was time for him to move on. The friend ended the conversation not knowing who consoled whom.

Dialogue of Steel

Larry could have chosen to be bitter about his firing, but he let it go. He sleeps better at nights and is not wasting any of his time holding onto grudges against people who are not wasting any time thinking about him.

Larry's Dialogue of Mush: I can't believe they fired me for no reason. This is so unfair.

Larry's Dialogue of Steel: Even though they fired me, maybe this is a blessing in disguise because I am meant to go in another direction.

Larry's DOM: But my life was fine before I was fired and I thought my job was going fine, too.

Larry's DOS: But I can't see what the future might hold. Perhaps this was not the best job for me after all. The more I judge, the more I will be held back from moving forward with my life.

Larry's DOM: Shouldn't I try to get even with them?

Larry's DOS: It is not for me to decide on their fate. If they unfairly hurt me, they must suffer those consequences, not me.

Larry's DOM: But I want revenge.

Larry's DOS: I don't want revenge. I choose life instead.

When you waste time hating someone, or holding a grudge, or wanting revenge, that is like taking poison and expecting someone else to get sick. Life is too short to judge. Every minute of your time is precious. Do not waste even one minute of your time thinking about the pain others have caused you. It is just not worth it.

Nuts And Bolts From Nerves Of Steel - The Penthouse Floor
Forgiveness, The Ultimate Strategy

No matter how much pain you have gone through in the past, either physical or mental, could your pain even approach the pain of someone like Viktor Frankl, who succumbed to the atrocities of concentration camps, losing almost his entire family in the process? So you can certainly forgive anyone who you feel has wronged you in the past.

You deserve better than to live your life worrying about gaining revenge on others, so it is now time to give up all grievances you are carrying for either past or present actions aimed toward yourself. Do you think people who you feel wronged you in the past are wasting their time thinking about you right now? Then why should you waste your precious time thinking about them?

Make the first move in forgiving each person you have held grudges against for maybe years or even decades and observe if you feel a giant weight has been lifted from your shoulders afterwards.

The more you are aware of your voluntary nerves, the more you can be aware of involuntary responses your mind puts your body through during times of duress or anger. Do you remember the most recent example of being angry at someone because of what you did?

Learning how to forgive is one of seven basic steps that you should keep in the forefront of your actions from day-to-day. Mother Theresa said that if you forgive, you will be set free.

How To Develop Nerves of Steel

Ordinary people can do extraordinary things by developing nerves of steel. If you adhere to these seven steps daily, you will be on your way to developing nerves of steel.

1) **Take Responsibility**
2) **Live Internally and Listen To the Cues Inside of You**
3) **Develop and Keep in Mind Your "68"**
4) **Find Out What You Want In Life and Give It Away**
5) **Change How You Feel and What You Feel by Changing What You Think**
6) **Let Go of Your Need to Always Be Right**
7) **Learn How To Forgive**

Adhering to these seven steps will guide you on your path to creating a "new you," a "you" that will stop wishing life was easier and teach you some important principles about how to get tougher on life, so life does not get tougher on you.

A beneficial method to ingrain the seven *Nerves of Steel* steps in your daily life is to think of ways to turn each step into a positive affirmation. Examples of such affirmations are as follows:

- I take responsibility for all my actions and their effects.
- I trust my intuition to positively guide me through my life.
- I have mapped out the guiding forces in my life and where I want them to take me.
- I strive to help other people achieve their dreams.
- I pay attention to what I think. I let good thoughts run rampant while squelching bad thoughts.

- If I am wrong, I freely admit it.
- I realize the importance of forgiving as the ultimate step in growing as a person.

Feel free to use the sample affirmations or to develop your own to more closely fit your journey toward your ultimate destination in life.

The last step, learning how to forgive, may be the most difficult of all the seven steps, because resentment has the ability to eat away at your soul like nothing else on earth. If you are resentful toward another person, you are taking poison and expecting that person to get sick.

You have only two resources on earth. If you think money is one of them, you are wrong. Your two resources are time and energy or good health. If you were on your death bed and the doctor came in and offered you one more year of life, pain-free, for a price, how much would you give?

Why should you waste what little time you have and expend much-needed energy on hating someone else? Chronic anger is one of the major causes of heart disease. Devote your time and energy to developing nerves of steel instead.

Developing nerves of steel is a never-ending process, just like producing steel is a never-ending manufacturing process.

You do not become healthy for life after one workout. Why would you think you can become motivated for life after reading one book, or attending one seminar, or accomplishing one goal?

When I do seminars, people often say that motivation wears off. I reply, "So does a bath, but I am not against taking them every day."

When the five o'clock whistle blows, a steel mill does not shut down and start back up again the next morning. The blast furnaces, machinery, and processes that run in a steel mill cannot just simply be shut down like a light switch and turned on the next day. Your life is the same way, a never-ending process. If you stay focused and keep stoking your coals of life, you will constantly produce steel, nerves of steel.

"68"

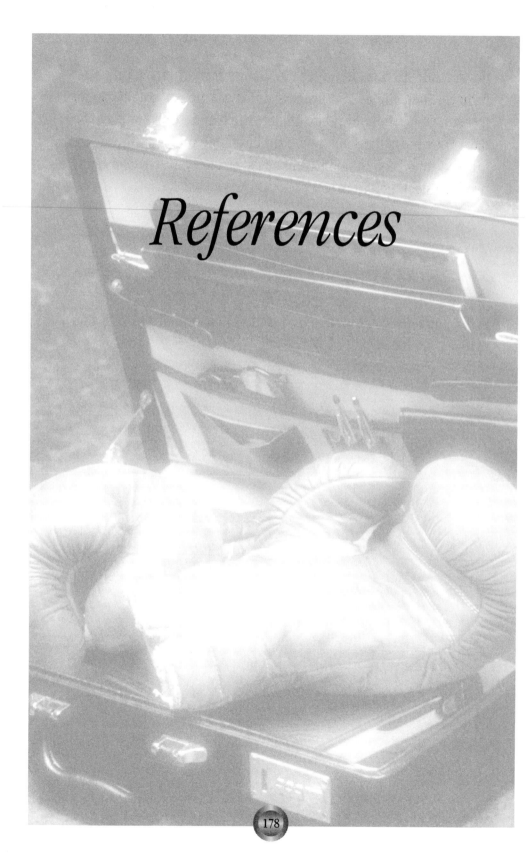

References

References

Introduction

McClelland, D. (1973). Testing for competence rather than intelligence. *American Psychologist, 28*, 1-14.

Floor 1

Bandura, A. (1986). *Social foundations of thought and action: A social-cognitive theory.* Englewood Cliffs, NJ: Prentice-Hall.

Baumeister, R.F. (1991). *Meanings of life.* New York: Guilford Press.

Fair, E.M., & Lynette, S. (1992). *Journal of Instructional Psychology, 19* (1), 3-8.

Endnotes

1. (1981, February). *Behavior Today*, p. 8.
2. Baumeister, R.F. (1991). *Meanings of life.* New York: Guilford Press.
3. Tucker-Ladd, C. *Psychological Self-Help.* http://www.mentalhealth.net/psy/help/.

Floor 2

Endnotes

1. Thoreau, H.D. *Cape cod.* Published in *Walden and other writings.* New York: Bantam Books. (1981).

Floor 3

Bird, L. (1989). *Drive.* New York: Bantam.

Scogin, F., Bynum, J., Stevens, G., & Calhoon, S. (1990). Efficacy of self administered treatment program: Meta-analytic review. *Professional Psychology: Research and Practice, 21*, 42-47.

Floor 4

Bandura, A. (1986). *Social foundations of thought and action: A Social-Cognitive Theory,* Englewood Cliffs, NJ: Prentice-Hall.

Ellis, A. (1988). *How to stubbornly refuse to make yourself miserable about anything - yes, anything.* Seacaucus, NJ: Lyle Stuart.

Gregory, R. L. (1970). *The Intelligent Eye.* New York: McGraw-Hill. From Coon, D. (1977). *Introduction To psychology.* St. Paul: West Publishing Company.

Hastorf, A., & Cantril, H. (1954). They saw a game: A case study. *Journal of Abnormal and Social Psychology, 49,* 129-134.

Turnbull, C.M. (1961). Some observations regarding the experiences and behavior of the Bambuti Pygmies. *American Journal of Psychology, 74,* 304-308.

Floor 5

Barkow, J., Cosmides, L., & Tooby, J. (1992) The *adapted mind: Evolutionary psychology and the generation of culture.* New York: Oxford University Press.

Dweck, C.S., & Licht. B. *Learned helplessness and intellectual achievement.* From Garber, J., & Seligman, M. (1980). *Human helplessness.* New York: Academic Press.

Fair, E.M., & Lynette, S. (1992). Effects of reward, competition, and outcome on intrinsic motivation. *Journal of Instructional Psychology, 19* (1), 3-8.

Floor 6

Kerr, G., & Gross, D. (1971). Personal control in elite gymnasts: The relationship between locus of control, self-esteem, and trait anxiety. *Journal Of Behavior, 20* (1), 69-72.

Santamaria, V, & Furst, D. (1957). Distance runners' causal attribution for most successful and least successful races. *Journal Of Sport Behavior, 1* (1), 43-51.

Floor 7

Frankl, V. (1963). *Man's search for meaning.* New York: Washington Square Press.

Homme, L. E. (1965). *Perspectives in psychology: XXIV.* Control of the coverants, the operants of the mind. *Psychological Record, 15,* 501-511.

Lazarus, R. S., & Folkman, S. (1984). *Stress, Appraisal and Coping.* New York: Springer.

Zimbardo, P.G. (1973). *Psychology and life (9th edition).* Glenview, Il: From Coon, D. (1977). *Introduction To Psychology.* St. Paul, MN:. West Publishing Company.

Floor 8

Horan, J.J. (1971). Coverant conditioning through a self-management application of the Premack Principle: Its effects on weight control. *Journal or Behavior Therapy and Experimental Psychiatry, 2,* 243-249.

Endnotes

1. Tucker-Ladd, C. *Psychological Self-Help.* http://www.mentalhelp.net/psy help/.

Penthouse

Ross, E.K. (1969). *On death and dying.* New York: Macmillian.

General References

Dreher, D. (1995). *The immune power personality.* New York: Penguin.

Ellis, A. (1979). *Discomfort anxiety: A new cognitive-behavioral construct.* Part 1. *Rational Living, 14* (2) 3-8.

Ellis, *A. (1978).* Treating the bored client with rational-emotive therapy. *Psychotherapy Patient, 3* (3-4), 75-86.

Ellis, A., & Knaus, W.J., (1977). *Overcoming procrastination.* New York: Signet.

Peterson, C., Maier S., & Seligman, M. (1993). *Optimism and bypass surgery, learned helplessness.* New York: Oxford University Press.

Rotter, J.B. Generalized expectancies for internal vs. external control of reinforcement, *Psychological Monographs, 80* (1), 609.